Why Women
Believe in God

Why Women Believe in God

Liz Hodgkinson

in conversation with sister Jayanti of the
Brahma Kumaris.

 Circle Books

Winchester, UK
Washington, USA

First published by Circle Books, 2012
Circle Books is an imprint of John Hunt Publishing Ltd., Laurel House, Station Approach,
Alresford, Hants, SO24 9JH, UK
office1@jhpbooks.net
www.johnhuntpublishing.com
www.circle-books.com

For distributor details and how to order please visit the 'Ordering' section on our website.

Design: Stuart Davies

Printed and bound by CPI Group (UK) Ltd, Croydon, CR0 4YY

We operate a distinctive and ethical publishing philosophy in all
areas of our business, from our global network of authors to
production and worldwide distribution.

CONTENTS

Introduction

1

Chapter One Women and Religion   8

Chapter Two Why and how women must lead the way   32

Chapter Three Science and Religion   54

Chapter Four I want a better world: where do I start?   79

Chapter Five How do I come to know God?   100

Chapter Six Who or what is God?   109

Chapter Seven More Awkward Questions Answered   126

Conclusion   141

Introduction

It used to be said that a book with the word God in the title would never sell. If that was true once, it is certainly not true now. Over the past few years books about God, both pro and anti, have become international bestsellers.

Two of the biggest successes in recent years have been no-holds-barred tomes on atheism: the uncompromisingly titled *The God Delusion*, by the Darwinist (and assiduous self-publicist) Richard Dawkins, and *God Is Not Great*, by the late Vanity Fair journalist Christopher Hitchens. Both of these books served to open up the God debate and encourage many people to think about subjects they had previously put firmly, and maybe permanently, on the back burner or, possibly, never thought about at all.

In his book, Dawkins argues forcefully that nowadays, science has supplanted superstition and with it, any lingering irrational belief in an eternal, supernatural creator, at least among the intelligent sections of society. Indeed, Dawkins goes so far as to say that anybody who continues to believe in God in the face of total lack of evidence for his existence or intervention in human affairs, is preternaturally stupid. Indeed, he has said that he would like all atheists to be known as 'brights'.

Dawkins has even gone so far as to design a range of atheist jewelry, available on his website, as a counter to all the crucifixes and Stars of David that religious people often wear. Maybe he said to himself: why should God have all the good jewelry?

Dawkins' polemic was followed up by Hitchens' entertainingly written diatribe, subtitled: How Religion Poisons Everything. Hitchens' argument was that the knotty ethical dilemmas have been solved far better by great writers than by religion, and that if we want answers to life, the universe and everything, we should turn to literature rather than the scriptures. Religion, continues Hitchens, spoke its last intelligible or inspiring words a long time ago and now has nothing whatever to offer us. He also maintains that religion was spread not because it was the true word of God but by so-called holy wars and imperialism.

Both of these books became international, angry bestsellers and then came another salvo, *Reflections on the God Debate*, by academic Terry Eagleton, writing from a Catholic and also, a Marxist, angle. This book was, if anything, even angrier and more entertaining than the Dawkins and Hitchens books.

Eagleton puts these two writers into a composite he calls Ditchkins and questions the supremacy of science and the scientific method over other means of enquiry and debate. Eagleton says that the new priestly caste of scientists has pretty much supplanted the previous priestly caste of priests, but does not accord them the reverence that Dawkins metes out to them. Indeed, Eagleton refers to science students at university as 'unspeakable yokels with dandruff on their collars'. He questions the Ditchkins notion that there is blind faith at one end of the scale and rational scientific evidence at the other, with nothing in between and argues that science and theology are simply not talking about the same things, so it is not very helpful to try and tie them together.

Since these books appeared, the ever-intensifying God debate has widened to include theologians, scientists, politicians, writers and even actors and comedians. Richard Dawkins has started an 'atheist' summer camp for children as a corrective to the religious, Bible-based summer camps, and British buses in London have carried the slogan: There is probably no God.

Brian Mountford, a vicar in Oxford, has added to the debate with his book, *Christian Atheist*, where he interviews people who wished they believed in God, and he makes the point that it is possible to follow Christian ethics without necessarily accepting the whole 'belief' package. David Bentley Hart, an American academic, has furthered the argument with his scholarly book, *Atheist Delusions*, which makes a strong case for Christianity, at least in its early stages, completely revolutionizing the world.

And now we, the present authors, are venturing to throw our hats has into the ring by arguing for a return to female-led spirituality. After all, both the atheist thinkers and the religious apologists have constituted a kind of boys' club where the protagonists throw mental, moral and scientific darts at each other, scoring points.

So, who are we, and what are our qualifications for writing about God?

One of us, Jayanti, is supremely qualified, having talked about little else for the past 40 years. She is a senior member of the Brahma Kumaris, the only spiritual organization of any significant size to be run and led by women. Starting in India in the 1930s, with just a handful of young women, it now has a presence in 130 countries.

I, like Christopher Hitchens, come from a British national newspaper background and am here to be persuaded, by the best evidence and arguments that can be mustered for God's existence and intervention in the world – or not, as the case may be.

Jayanti was born in India but educated at British schools and London University. Since the age of 19, she has dedicated herself to spiritual practice and has lived the life of a modern nun by renouncing any kind of personal life, and spending much time in meditation and contemplation.

I, by contrast, have unashamedly dedicated my life to Mammon, having lived a secular life to the full with a big career, several relationships, a marriage, children and many different homes. I am also a lover of fashion, fine food, interiors, films, books, cinema and theatre. As one of my sons succinctly put it: "Mum would always rather have her nails done than ponder the eternal verities."

However, on many important issues Jayanti and I, who have been friends for over 30 years, agree with each other. We are both in accord, for instance – and who could not be – that in all the major religions, Hinduism, Buddhism, Judaism, Christianity and Islam, women have been shamefully marginalized and repressed, treated as second class citizens all the way. In all the main world religions, men have been placed far above women. Even in pagan myths and legends, the head, overall God is always a man, or the male principle.

And in Middle Eastern religions, the angels and archangels, Gabriel, Raphael, Michael and so on, plus the heavenly hosts of cherubim and seraphim, are all understood to be male. The leading prophets, Abraham, Jesus and Mohammed, are male as well. Never in the whole history of religion, has God called upon a female to interpret His word to the rest of the world.

Religions have always repressed women and stamped down on any notion of equality, so one of the first dilemmas we ponder is: why should intelligent, educated women of today give spirituality any credence?

Jayanti and I also agree that it was not until secularization in the twentieth century, when religions began to lose their stranglehold, that women began to be educated in any significant numbers and were gradually accorded equal rights with men.

Another factor is that it was not until the demise of religion that rigid class structures in society began to be dismantled. The French and Russian Revolutions secularized and equalized society by getting rid of the Kings, Queens, Czars and Czarinas. Turkey became a secular state under Kemal Ataturk and the rise of the proletariat and the demise of the aristocracy in many countries, including India, was part and parcel of the formation of a Godless or should we say, secular, society.

In the days when religions held powerful sway, it was not just women, but certain men who were considered inferior to others. India had its rigid caste system, Russia had serfs and in other parts of the world, slavery was not only allowed but encouraged, by many religions. Imperialism brought Christianity and Islam to many parts of the world, in order to subjugate the 'subject' races. It was not until the 1950s and 60s, when secularization was far advanced in the world, that the concept of equal rights for all races began to take hold.

So far, so good. Secularization has brought about much equality and loosening of class structures and gender differences. Yet at the same time as secularization has advanced, so have pockets of fundamentalism and also, as it seems, has rampant greed and dishonesty unleashed, on a scale never known before.

The secular age has been characterized by many things but the spread of love, kindness, compassion, truth, justice, respect for others, and altruism, have not been amongst them. Indeed, the virtues traditionally expounded by all religions, at least at their core, have been remarkably absent from the secular society. Instead of becoming unselfish, we have become more selfish than ever. Maybe we have been influenced by a previous book by Richard Dawkins and also a bestseller in its day, *The Selfish Gene.*

The secular wars fought in the twentieth century have been more violent, more bloody than any previous ones fought in the name of religion, and a new thing has happened, in that civilians are now involved as much as the armed forces.

There is now more cruelty, more violence, more drug taking, more family breakdown, more murders, more serial killings, than at any time in history, and this is affecting ever more people. In Tudor times, according to historian John Bellamy, premeditated murder hardly ever happened. Nowadays, novels about planned crimes and murder, known as 'thrillers' are among the most popular and widely read genres in the world. At the cinema, films are becoming ever more violent. Indeed, the more violent the film, the greater, often, is its box office success. Pornography is widely available, and small children can easily access hardcore porn on the internet.

There is more devastation of the planet than ever before and thanks to advances in science, we now have the means for a total holocaust, with many more weapons of mass destruction than in 1945, when the first atomic bombs were dropped.

Many of our treasured institutions have been revealed to be greedy, abusive, self-seeking and rotten to the core. Journalist Charlie Booker, writing in the British newspaper *The Guardian* in July 2009, had this to say:

> *You can't move for toppling institutions. Television, the economy, the police, the House of Commons and, most recently, the press – all revealed to be jam-packed with liars and bastards and graspers and bullies and turds.*
>
> *Right now, all our faith has poured out of the old institutions and there's nowhere left to put it. We need new institutions to believe in, and fast.*

Whatever the truth or otherwise of the Ditchkins stance, nobody can argue with any of the above. It is self-evident and every day seems to bring news of new awfulness on a scale unknown before. Banks are losing billions of dollars of customers' money, systematic child abuse has been uncovered in many sections of the Catholic priesthood and the British mother of parliaments, long respected in the rest of the world, has been shown to consist of politicians with their hands deeply and firmly in the public purse.

In 2011, the earth itself rebelled, with earthquakes, hurricanes, tsunamis, floods and other natural disasters never before witnessed on such a scale, or following on so fast from one another.

So will God, having been brushed aside for so long, now reveal himself (or herself) and usher in a new Golden Age such as poets since classical times have predicted? Or will the unstoppable greed, selfishness and violence that characterizes our present age lead to mass destruction?

Or, alternatively, can we, as Ditchkins asserts, bring in the age of gold without recourse to a supernatural, non-material being?

One thing is certain: we can no longer leave it to men. It is now time for women to take their rightful place and to lead, rather than follow. The means and methods by which this can be achieved and by which we can bring back values in society, are described in this book. We also outline how and why women have been marginalized by old-style religions, and why a return to traditional faiths can never be the answer.

Finally, we will describe a new concept of God that does not depend on either evolutionary or creationist theory, but which provides a brand-new, workable, way of looking at things and moving forward with strength and optimism.

It is a concept based on the female, or feminine, principle of harmony and connectedness, rather than the masculine principle of divide, rule and conquer. The old ways no longer serve us and as the seventeenth-century poet John Dryden wrote: *Tis well an old age was out/And time to begin a new.*

Because many of the concepts and ideas propounded in this book will be startling and unfamiliar, we have used a Question and Answer format. This will enable me, as the 'ordinary reader' and sometimes, Devil's Advocate, to ask the awkward questions and Jayanti to answer them from a spiritual, feminine perspective.

Chapter One

Women and Religion

The late Finnish lawyer, Helvi Sipila, champion of women's rights at the United Nations, was fond of saying that although half the world was 'found' by Christopher Columbus in 1492, it took the world another 500 years to 'find' the other half – women.

According to Silipa, women were discovered, for all practical purposes, in Mexico in 1975, when the UN's first International Year for Women was held, and this sparked off the UN Decade for Women in 1976. From that date, definite targets began to be set to secure equal access for women to education, employment, promotion, political participation, healthcare, housing, nutrition and contraception.

It is now unarguably the case that those countries where women are found at high levels in government, industry and the professions, such as Scandinavia, are the most advanced in the world. By contrast, the most backward and uncivilised states are all controlled by men.

So why did it take so long and need such a special effort for the world to recognise women as people in their own right? After all, or so one assumes, women have been around just as long as men.

Step forward, religion, and hang your head in shame.

One of the most distressing aspects of organised religion, and in particular the five main world religions of Hinduism, Buddhism, Judaism, Christianity and Islam, is the way they have without exception marginalised and oppressed women throughout the ages. Since the inception of these religions, women have been considered inferior to men and not worthy of the same treatment. For centuries this was seen as the natural order of things, enshrined in Holy Writ and therefore the word of God.

It was not even questioned until very late in the world's history.

There has never been any gender equality in any of the main religions or their many offshoots, and probably never will be while these religions continue to wield any power or influence. Even nowadays, every time an evangelical or fundamentalist branch of a particular religion surfaces or gains power, women are instantly relegated back to secondary, subordinate positions. We have seen this with the Taliban and other terrorist groups operating in the name of religion, where girls' schools have been closed down or bombed, and women ordered back in to the burqa, on pain of death, and even punished for being raped.

There was also, in July 2009, a shameful case in the Sudan where 13 women were arrested for wearing trousers in a restaurant, and sentenced to 10 lashes and a £65 fine each for 'indecent dress'. Ten of the women accepted the sentence, but three challenged it and brought the case to court, when it became an international incident. The so-called decency laws are supposed to originate in the Koran, but one of the women, journalist and UN worker Lubna Hussein, said, "It is not about religion. It is about men treating women badly." Although the Sudanese ambassador in London wrote to newspapers saying that the women were not being punished for indecent dress but for loud and lewd behaviour, their barbaric punishment indicates the low esteem in which women are held in that country.

This particular incident happened to come to international attention, but it is by no means an isolated occurrence. Throughout the ages, men have taken it upon themselves to dictate suitable dress and behaviour for women in the name of religion, yet it has never happened the other way round.

In her book *She For God*, an overview of the way women have been treated and regarded in Christianity, Katharine Moore writes that at the time of Christ, women in the so-called civilized world were little better than slaves. And although there were a few redoubtable female characters depicted in the Old Testament of the Bible, such as Ruth, Judith, Esther and Naomi, and also in Greek tragedy, these people, whether real or fictional, had little or no influence on the low status of women generally. In Judaism, the law was taught only to boys and few Jewish girls were even taught how to read.

In a court of law, no Jewish woman was ever considered to be a reliable witness.

In classical times, Aristotle believed women were basically slaves and inferior to men in moral, physical and intellectual power. It was even doubtful, in many traditions, as to whether women possessed souls or were properly human. In Roman law, the woman was always in the power of a man, whether father, husband or brother, and she had no rights over her own children. This law was to persist in the West until the end of the nineteenth century, when theories about mother/child bonding began to have influence, after which mothers were usually awarded custody.

Although women played a significant part in the spread of early Christianity, this did not last long and they were soon supplanted by men in every position of power and influence. Early female Christians could be martyrs and thrown to the lions, but were never allowed to be priests or take holy orders. When the Normans conquered Britain, they did not allow women to inherit property, a law that remains in place to this day, at least where great estates are concerned. Women were never allowed to be Queens or Heads of State in any European country, except by default when there was no male heir. With the rise of Puritanism and Protestantism, the denigration of women increased, and the many witchcraft trials all over Europe found mainly women guilty of being witches. It was very rare that a man was burned at the stake as a witch.

By Victorian times, the status of women had sunk even lower, if possible, than before and the patriarchal family unit assumed more importance than ever. One remembers the great nineteenth-century writer Charles Dickens, the champion of the downtrodden, drawing up a Deed of Separation between him and his wife Catherine, after she had borne him ten children, and banishing her from his and their children's lives. And there was absolutely nothing she could have done about it; he held all the power and she had none. This is not an isolated incident, but just one of the more famous examples of the way women could be discarded by their husbands.

By this time, the education of girls was practically non-existent, although there were at this time, paradoxically, many female missionaries and women hymn writers coming to the fore. Hymns written by Mrs Cecil Alexander (*All Things Bright and Beautiful; There is a Green Hill Far Away*) by Christina Rossetti (*In the Deep Midwinter*), by Julia Ward Howe (*The Battle Hymn of the Republic*) and by Eleanor Farjeon (*Morning Has Broken* –and no you at the back there, it was NOT written by Cat Stevens) have become world-famous.

Many hymns written by women have a tenderness and universal appeal which is not found so frequently in hymns written by men, and show that women have a deep and abiding appreciation of the spiritual, once allowed to express it.

But generally speaking and with very few exceptions, women were not accorded any real importance by religion, and this was encoded and enforced in civil and criminal law. Until very recently, most of a country's laws governing behaviour were based on religious laws taken from the scriptures.

It was not until some brave women unconnected with religion started to say: Hey, wait a minute; what about us, that things began to change, very slowly and painfully at first, and gradually, the entrenched order which had militated against all women for so many centuries, began to be questioned.

The first women who dared to raise a voice in protest at their secondary status, the suffragettes and early educationalists at the end of the nineteenth century were shouted down for being 'unfeminine', even by women, and had a mighty struggle to have a voice, let alone any power or access to education, the professions or earning their own living. Queen Victoria famously inveighed against 'women's rights' which were just beginning to be asserted towards the end of her long reign. Women were often far from being champions of other women, although it is mainly thanks to campaigning females that women were gradually allowed to train as doctors, lawyers and academics, and stand for election in Parliament.

These early feminists had a long way to go – maybe nobody appreciated just how far - and the battle is far from over, as inequality continues to be deeply embedded in every single society, thanks to the baleful influence of traditional religions, all of which have had men at their head and a largely or entirely male priesthood. Even in 2012, every single head of a traditional religion is a man. A religious programme on British television shown in August 2009 interviewed the heads of the five main religions operating in the UK – Christianity, Islam, Judaism, Buddhism and Hinduism – and every one was a man. Where are the female representatives of these world religions? Even nowadays, pretty much nowhere.

If we take a look at one of the most fundamental aspects of any society, legal arrangements for the pairing of males and females, we will find that the institution of marriage, which joins men and women together in both a religious and a secular contract, has never been an equal compact between the two sexes.

Instead, the woman has always been treated as the lesser, inferior half of the coupling, to be subsumed into the male half of the partnership. On marriage, the woman has, in very many societies, been effectively buried alive, and never allowed to leave the house, at least on her own. Laws and customs have put her in a moated grange as secure as any prison. Many religions have hailed marriage as a sacrament and in the Church of England in particular, the marriage service is enshrined in the Book of Common Prayer. But it has always been a sacrament which has instantly put the woman in the inferior position.

Just to give a few examples: on marriage a woman has widely been expected to take the man's surname and lose her own. Although in England and America this was never an actual law, it was a custom so strong that women had to fight – and still do have to fight – to retain their 'own' names after marriage. Most did not, until very recently, keep their own surnames but were content to be known by their husband's surname, as this implied increased status.

In Victorian times, many female novelists felt they had to go by male names in order to get published and noticed – George Eliot in the UK and George Sand in France are famous examples – and other female novelists went by their husband's names; Mrs Henry Wood being the prime example.

Indeed, so famous in her lifetime did Mrs Henry Wood become that her unknown husband used to introduce himself in public gatherings as 'Mr Mrs Henry Wood.'

Again, in most societies the spinster, divorcee, widow or otherwise unmarried or unattached woman has had a lesser status than her married sister, and in some societies to be unmarried was almost a sin in itself.

In many Eastern societies, it was actually impossible for a woman not to be married. There was no such thing as a single woman, as all girls were forced into an arranged marriage at the age of 13 or 14 or even younger, even if the marriage was not actually consummated until later. It will be remembered that Mahatma Gandhi was married by arrangement at the age of 13; his bride was the same age. If there were not enough men to go round then several women could be legally married to the same man, and for very rich men there was the tradition of the harem; again, few if any women have ever had a 'harem' of men at their exclusive disposal.

And woe betide any member of the harem who disobeyed her husband. Polygamy has a present-day echo in the practices of some Mormons but again, few if any Mormon women have more than one husband. However you dress them up, marriage laws come down to the basic fact of men being in charge of women. The wedding dress symbolises a sacrificial lamb; a notion many modern women would dispute when they order their expensive meringues, but it is there all the same.

This extract from the American magazine *Good Housekeeping* of May 13,1955 says it all:

Have dinner ready. Plan ahead, even the night before, to have a delicious meal ready, on time, for his return. This is a way of letting him know that you have been thinking about him and are concerned about his needs. Most men are hungry when they come home and the prospect of a good meal (especially his favourite dish) is part of the warm welcome needed.

Gather up schoolbooks, toys, paper etc and then run a dustcloth over the tables.

Be happy to see him.

Greet him with a warm smile and show sincerity in your desire to please him. ,

Listen to him. You may have a dozen important things to tell him, but the moment of his arrival is not the time. Let him talk first – remember, his topics of conversation are more important than yours.

Don't complain if he's late home for dinner or even if he stays out all night. Count this as minor compared to what he might have gone through that day.

Arrange his pillow and offer to take off his shoes. Speak in a low, soothing and pleasant voice.

Don't ask him questions about his actions or question his judgment or integrity. Remember, he is the master of the house and as such will always exercise his will with fairness and truthfulness. You have no right to question him.

A good wife always knows her place.

Come in, Betty Friedan!

Another aspect of the traditional, embedded inequality of marriage was the frequent huge disparity of ages. Again in Eastern and Middle Eastern societies, it was not at all unusual for girls or 13 or 14 to be married to a man in his 40s or 50s; it hardly ever happened the other way round. The half-English Jehan Sadat was married at 15, yes, 15, to Anwar el-Sadat, who became Egypt's Head of State. He was in his thirties and had been married before. Until fairly recently, nobody questioned the concept of the child bride. The idea here, whether stated or implied, was to put the woman into a forced and inescapable situation before she had grown up or known any other life, so that she could not then become dissatisfied.

This custom, that the man has to be much older than the woman, persisted in British, European and American society until very recently. It will be remembered that Princess Diana was barely 20 when she married Prince Charles who was 12 years older. Diana's mother Frances was married at 18 to a man of 33, and this was considered an 'ideal' age gap. Frances's own mother, Ruth, Lady Fermoy, was married at 20 to a man of 46. Nobody thought this was at all odd; nor was it considered remotely strange that the man was almost always better educated than the woman who very often, would have no education at all other than at a Swiss finishing school if her parents were very rich.

In British society until the early 1960s there was the tradition of the debutantes, where parents of young girls of 17 or 18 would hold balls or dances for the express purpose of putting their daughters on show to meet their marriage partner in one, or at the most, two, seasons. Again, these girls from the highest echelons of the aristocracy would be uneducated and completely unfit to earn their own living. They were bred for marriage, and marriage only – but never to be an equal partner.

So far as dissolving the marriage was concerned, this was held to be a sin and a disgrace. Princess Margaret, the Queen's sister, was not allowed to marry her first lover, Group Captain Peter Townsend, because he was a divorcé. Further back, the fact that Mrs Simpson had been divorced twice put it way beyond any possibility that she might become Queen of England. Indeed, until the 1970s the Church of England would not marry or even give a blessing to couples if one or both of the partners had been divorced.

In Christianity, it was held that marriage was indissoluble, even though the Church of England had been founded because of a divorce – that of Henry VIII and Catherine of Aragon. The new Church then immediately turned itself into the arbiter of marital behaviour. In traditional Catholicism, marriage was also indissoluble although it could sometimes be annulled for non-consummation.

In Islam, divorce was not considered a sin, but only the man could instigate this separation. It was the same in Judaism, and it remains the case in ultra-Orthodox Judaism that only the man can instigate a divorce. In traditional Hinduism, it is still considered very shameful for a woman to be divorced; less so for a man.

Religion also governed sexual behaviour. In Christianity, and many other religions, women were supposed to be virgins on marriage. Traditionally men were supposed to be virgins as well, but the rules here were always less strict, as the male desire to sow wild oats was frequently indulged. The fact that he would have to sow them with another woman, often a prostitute or concubine, was never really taken into consideration. Women were put on earth for one purpose only; to serve men, either as wives, mothers or prostitutes or in some cases, to be muses for their talent or genius. The man who encouraged and fostered a woman's talent was so rare as to be almost non-existent; in fact in the whole history of fiction, only two examples spring to mind: George Henry Lewes who devoted himself to the talent of Marian Evans, known as George Eliot, and Leonard Woolf, who championed the work of his wife Virginia.

The worlds of music, painting and architecture reveal even fewer examples.

One major reason why women in traditional societies were married off at such a young age is that they would not then have the opportunity to become sexually experienced before marriage, and therefore able to compare performance. Of course, the younger they were married, the more children they could have and it was not unknown for women to have a dozen or more children.

The Rev Sabine Baring-Gould, perhaps best remembered nowadays as author of the hymn *Onward Christian Soldiers,* married an 18-year old mill girl, Grace Taylor, and proceeded to have 15 children. A story is told of him coming into a children's party at his house and asking one child: "And whose little girl are you?" She replied, "I'm one of yours, Daddy."

But while Grace was busy producing baby after baby, her husband sat in his study and produced book after book, some of them bestsellers in their day. Their marriage has been described as a 'great success', but where was the equality?

The traditional religions also took it upon themselves to govern sexual behaviour in other ways. In Christianity, Hinduism, Islam and Judaism, women were not supposed to have sex before marriage, and afterwards they were compelled to. In Islam and Hinduism, a woman can never refuse her husband and in Christian countries, there was no such crime as rape within marriage until the 1980s; this new law was instigated only after intense campaigning by women.

In many religions, contraception was considered wicked and abortion was a crime. A woman who killed her baby after being seduced or raped by a man, could be hanged. In George Eliot's novel *Adam Bede*, Hetty Sorrel is originally sentenced to be hanged for murdering her baby – a baby she never wanted anyway – but her sentence was eventually transmuted to transportation to Australia.

The man of course, both in real life and in fiction, got away scot-free and was never brought to justice.

Much of this is well known and has been picked over by many feminist writers, but it is not always appreciated just how much women's low status was entirely due to the stranglehold of religion.

Education was another contentious issue and almost always left women less well off than men. In most societies until recently, only boys were considered worthy of being educated. It was the custom, again in many countries, for a girl to stay at home until she was chosen by some man to be his bride, when she would go and live in her husband's house or, in Indian societies, in the house of the husband's family. There was no choice, no freedom of movement and in most cases, no escape from the life sentence of marriage.

Although in Christianity the church instigated many admirable educational institutions, for centuries these were for males only. England's world-famous old-established public schools such as Eton, Harrow, Westminster and Winchester, were for centuries institutions solely for boys; there was no female equivalent until women like Miss Beale and Miss Buss pioneered equivalent female education in the 19th century. Although these admirable women ushered in higher education for girls, with the founding of Cheltenham Ladies' College and the North London Collegiate School, they were widely lampooned for being sexless spinsters, as in the music-hall rhyme:

Miss Buss and Miss Beale
Cupid's darts do not feel.
How different from us,
Miss Beale and Miss Buss.

The old-established universities of Oxford and Cambridge, both originally founded by the Church in the 12th century to train young men for the priesthood, did not admit women until the late nineteenth century, and it was not until the 1940s that women graduates of Cambridge were allowed degrees on the same basis as men.

In the 1960s, less than 10 per cent of the students at Cambridge were women.

In fact, whenever religion has been behind an institution, you can bet that women were not allowed at all, or were admitted only very reluctantly.

Religions also tried its level best to prevent women from having any money of their own. In India, the dowry is a sum of money the parents pay the man's family to take the woman off their hands. Although traditionally the dowry was supposed to be the woman's wealth, for her own use, this almost never happened and the woman was left stranded, without any education, training or access to money, completely at the mercy of her husband. Any money or property belonging to women in Britain was considered their husband's until the Married Woman's Property Act came into force in 1882. Even as late as the 1960s, women in the UK were not allowed to sign a hire purchase agreement or a mortgage document unless they had a male guarantor.

Until the end of the nineteenth century, women were not allowed to enter any of the main professions and even then it was considered such a privilege to allow them to earn a living that they had to relinquish this immediately on marriage. Then of course there was the fact that women were not allowed to vote for members of parliament in many countries; there is still not complete equality here.

Religion, too, traditionally regarded women, although not men, as 'unclean'. The Old Testament of the Bible refers to women being 'unclean' during menstruation, and any man who has sex with her during this time was also regarded as 'unclean', although always for a shorter time. The idea that menstruation, a normal and natural function which is completely unstoppable before the menopause except by hysterectomy, is a mark of shame, is also echoed in many religions. Hinduism and Islam have taken it upon themselves to prevent women taking part in certain activities during their time of the month. They are not allowed in many Hindu and Jain temples during this time, and the underlying idea of this is that if they take part in everyday activities, they may pollute the men.

Then childbirth, again unpreventable until effective contraception was given a reluctant blessing, was in itself considered an unclean act. It was women's intimate association with blood and bleeding which made them 'unclean' in the eyes of the holy men of the church, and therefore, subject to strict behavioural taboos. Menstruation was of course, something that very much set women apart from men and this difference was considered to render them naturally inferior. In the 1970s, writer Gloria Steinem addressed this centuries-old taboo with an article: *If Men Could Menstruate*. If they could, she wrote, this act would become celebrated and ritualised, instead of hidden away in shame. But because it is confined to women only, it is considered proof of women's weakness and inferiority.

These are just a few of the more glaring ways in which women have been considered inferior to men and not worthy of equal treatment. And in most cases, these laws were encoded in religions and religious observances.

Mostly, it has to be said, women colluded in their own oppression, and in turn oppressed other women. Maybe, with no access to education, money or independence, they simply did not see any choice in the matter. Women, practically universally, preferred to have male babies than to reproduce their own sex, and viewed the birth of a girl as an abject failure. In many societies, the insistence on producing a male heir, at least when there was money or inheritance at stake – led to women producing lots of unwanted girls. Just two examples will suffice: Frances, the mother of Princess Diana, produced three girls before eventually giving birth to the present Earl Spencer, and Lady Lambton had six or seven daughters, including the TV personality Lucinda, before finally producing a male heir. Princess Diana herself was luckier; she quickly produced two boys and did not then have to have any more children.

In India, this preference continues with wrong-sex abortion and in the present day Punjab, there are now around four males to every female, the direct result of aborting female foetuses, even though the practice is supposed to be illegal.

Throughout all societies and all ages, women were kept down by religion, and it was only the advent of secularisation which changed all this. Both the French and the Russian Revolutions were motivated by secularism and were avowedly anti-church. As a result of these revolutions and the overturning of the kings and czars, society began to be more equal and with it, there was at least some emancipation of women. The church, especially the Catholic church, insisted on and continued, a rigid male hierarchy which was supposed to be divinely ordained. In Britain, the concept of the Divine Right of Kings continued until Cromwell's time, when the monarchy was temporarily overturned. But the ancient concept of Kings being divinely ordained and appointed continues with the British Queen being defined as Fidei Defensor; Defender of the Faith.

And of course the British Queen is only Queen by default, through lack of male heirs, as was the case in Holland and Denmark.

Although there is some way to go, it is only since religion, with its insistence on a rigid and unalterable structure of society, began to lose its hold, that women have started to come to the fore in all aspects of public life and have belatedly begun to take charge of their own destiny.

In the West at least, women do not now have to marry in order to survive, but can earn their own living and be completely independent of a man, or men. This is completely new in the history of the world. There are now at least as many women as men at university in Western countries, and women have access to all professions. Although there are still not equal numbers in the higher reaches of most professions, at least women now have a significant presence.

Traditional religions have treated women very badly indeed, no argument, and yet if you go into a Christian church anywhere in the world, you will see that around 75% of the congregation is always women. And Jayanti maintains that it is women who now have to lead the way in bringing the world back to spirituality and a spiritual understanding.

Sister Jayanti agrees that religion has treated women badly all over the world but still believes that women must now lead the way back to spirituality and a Godly way of life.

What are her reasons?

Why do you believe women are marginalised in every single religion?

In the Adam and Eve story, which provides the basis of the Bible, Torah and Koran, the story goes that God, being man, created Man in his own image and woman out of the Man's rib. This makes her instantly a second class citizen and the idea that the direct creation was man, and that the woman came out of man has an echo in many scriptures and is one of the main reasons why women have always been treated as lesser beings than men.

Another factor is that in the Bible, Eve tempted Adam and this makes her responsible for all the sin in the world. The story of Pandora's Box is a version of the same story and underlines the idea that all the evil in the world comes from woman, not man.

These myths were of course written long after the supposed event and they were written to support the patriarchal society. For centuries, nobody argued with this as it was seen as the Divine Order of things. In all monotheistic religions, God is seen as male, and man his direct creation, but in polytheistic religions the situation is not much different; where there are Gods and Goddesses, the head God is still always a male figure, or a male principle.

In primitive societies without a sophisticated religion, the man, being the hunter, was seen as the breadwinner, and the function of women was creating and looking after children.

So, in most societies, women were automatically lesser creatures and this was enshrined in every codified religion.

In many societies, women are either deified and put on a pedestal, as with the Virgin Mary in Christianity, or are seen as temptresses, such as Mary Magdalene. It is the same in Hinduism. In the very origins of religion, the woman has never been portrayed as an equal and so can never have an equal relationship with a man. A woman is never a normal creature taking an equal position with males, but is either a prostitute or a virgin.

In Christianity, the people coming to Jesus were all men. Which woman was allowed to follow Christ? Jesus did not select a female disciple and the Christian church has always upheld this as the main reason why only men should be ordained priests. The idea of the apostolic succession is enshrined in Catholicism which to this day, has no female priests.

In the Church of England, there is huge outcry every time the subject of female bishops crops up, and many adherents either threaten to become Catholic or actually do so, in protest. There are no women at the head of any traditional religion or church.

I met Mother Teresa several times and when I saw her in Kilburn, London, in the early 1990s, the priest was a young man in his twenties and she had to kneel at his feet. Here was Mother Teresa, an elderly, world-famous woman, widely considered a saint, and she was still subservient to the priest. The power of women has simply never been acknowledged in traditional religions.

In India, the person leading the congregation is either a sage or a priest but in any case is always male.

Women have never been considered equal from the very start of written scriptures, yet in at least three of the main religions, Judaism, Hinduism and Christianity, the woman carries on the tradition of the sacred by teaching the children how to pray and read the scriptures. It is so often the woman who carries on and instigates the tradition of the sacred even though it is so dominated by men.

In Hinduism for example, it is always the woman who keeps the shrine in the house and offers flowers to the Gods, never the man. And yet, in India women were not even permitted to read the scriptures as it was generally felt they were incapable of understanding them. In India also, women were prevented from worshipping Shiva as this God was seen as a phallic symbol, a symbol of power.

Women, as I see it, have been the sustainers and nurturers of religion because they were not out in the world and did not have to give time to earning. Instead, they gave space and time to introspection and if religion is to have any meaning, this is a requirement.

It was the case in Christianity, that women often did lead the way. Many of the early Christians were women and many were martyred for their beliefs. Early Christian woman often showed incredible fortitude and bravery for their beliefs, and helped to further the spread of Christianity. Later on, female Quakers were persecuted and tortured for their beliefs. There are very many Christian female saints, most of whom were martyred or tortured, so it was allowable to die for one's beliefs but never to be in charge in any way.

Why have women meekly put up with men being in charge?

For centuries, even women have discriminated against girls, in very many societies. I remember that when I was eleven, my mother would call me in from playing outside to help her make chapattis. Yet my brother was never called; he was allowed to stay out and play. When I asked her why, she said that my brother would never have to make chapattis. The cultural context was so strong she could not even imagine my younger brother ever cooking and yet now in his own home, he does all the cooking!

There has never been equal treatment of boys and girls in the home until very recently. It is true that women have colluded in their own oppression and this has been more than anything for the purposes of survival. Unless the woman kowtowed to the man, she would have no way of surviving.

In India until the 1980s, if the mother gave special attention to the son and he acknowledged this, he was more likely to look after her in her old age. The daughter in law might like or hate her mother in law but she had no choice but to accept her. In this way, women could ensure they were being taken care of all their lives. Within the home the mother became the matriarchal figure and it was in her own interests to look after her son.

In Hinduism, it was never an option for women to reject family life. There was simply no alternative for them, no possible other way for them to survive. It has been a similar story in Islam. In the West, Catholicism and some branches of Protestantism traditionally had an alternative to home life for women in that they could become nuns, but nuns were never considered a part of normal society.

There was also in Hinduism, no possibility of married women refusing their husband conjugal rights. This was totally embedded in society and when in the 1930s, female members of the Om Mandli, the forerunner of the Brahma Kumaris, refused sex with their husbands, the case came to court. The young woman then at the Head of the Institution, Om Radhe, known as Mama, had to face all these British barristers and judges in court, and she stated that the women had sacrificed family life for their love of God. The judges found for the Om Mandli, and this was a historical judgment which gave women choice for the very first time in India.

My own conviction is that although men have been upholders and leaders in every major religion without exception, women are more naturally spiritual and this is why, now, it is up to women to lead the way. Another point is that if people are oppressed and there is nobody to help you, the natural inclination is to turn towards God.

This was the case with African slaves in America. Very quickly, they became Christians and set up their own churches. The idea also has an echo in the book *The Color Purple*, made into a film by Steven Spielberg, where the black heroine, Celie, is so very alone she has nobody to write to but God.

Is religion, then, the opium of the people?

What happened, as I see it, is that eventually religion and the monarchy became so corrupt and self-serving that the kings, czars and emperors were overthrown and religion along with it. Religion was seen very much as part of a society which treated people unequally and this was never going to change without a revolution. Religion, the monarchy and the aristocracy were not going to relinquish their power voluntarily, and so had to be overthrown forcibly.

What happened, and nobody can deny this, is that the religion of many countries was overthrown and as a direct result, a more equal society came in.

From 1975 I started attending women's conferences all over the world and one I particularly remember in East Germany showcased how wonderful opportunities in the Eastern bloc had opened up for women. At that time, the government provided crèches which were unheard of in the UK. They were mandatory, and allowed women to have senior professional positions. When I went to Russia for the first time, I was amazed at how many female doctors, engineers, professors and politicians there were; it was far ahead of anything in the West at the time.

What I witnessed in Russia and Eastern bloc countries in those days supports the argument that in all religions women were considered second class citizens and yet when the world started to be secularised, opportunities opened up for women everywhere.

It happened in India as well. Nehru, India's first prime minister, came from the highest reaches of society. He was a Pandit, yet when he became premier he made India a secular country, from conscious choice. Nehru decided that religion was preventing progress and he had this vision of a modern, industrialised India. Throughout the 1950s India pursued secularism and had Russia as an ally and a friend. For the very first time, women were educated in significant numbers – all thanks to the policy of secularisation.

Traditionally, schools and universities were religious foundations and as such, only for men. This was so in the West but was also the case in India.

In 1988, I travelled to Russia for the first time. This was the time of Gorbachev and I was given strict instructions not to mention God on any account. I was there to give a lecture on meditation and my brief was to talk about the impact of meditation on the mind. Religion had held such sway in Russia until the Revolution that after secularisation, people had to be forcibly prevented from adhering to any religion, as this would impede progress, as it was popularly thought.

What about marriage and divorce?

Within every society – or at least the majority of cultures – women have had to sacrifice their past lives on marriage. In India women get a new first and second name on marriage but this does not happen with the man. The woman sacrifices everything but the opposite is never true. In no society, whether primitive or sophisticated, has marriage ever been an equal contract between men and women. In desert societies where women may not be able to find a man, there is the situation of polygamy. There has always been the idea that all women have to be married, and that any unmarried or single woman is a 'spare' woman or a 'useless mouth'.

How do women fare in an unequal society?

In all societies where women have been considered inferior to men, it has been the woman who has suffered most. Women have never had equal access to finances, healthcare or political power, and have had to put up with the way men behaved. For instance, detractors of religion have stated that most of the wars in the past were fought for religious reasons, yet modern wars have not been religious, and they have been the most bloody, brutal and violent wars in history.

Also, modern wars involve civilians just as much as the armed forces and it is usually women and children, the most helpless members of society, who bear the brunt of these wars. Just to give one stark example: on 6th and 9th August 1945 the US dropped atomic bombs on the Japanese cities of Hiroshima and Nagasaki. In Hiroshima, around 180,000 people were killed out of a population of 350,000 and in Nagasaki, around 100,000 people were killed from a population of 240,000. In both cases, the overwhelming majority of people killed were civilians, ordinary men, women and children. The children of survivors were often born with genetic deformities, cancers or intestinal problems.

This was not a religious war, but the end of World War Two. In the Gaza Strip, the world was horrified by pictures of dead children being laid out on the street during the conflict of January and February 2009.

Although women have been treated very badly by every major religion, we are reaching a situation where we have no spiritual values at all, and everything once considered spiritual has become debased.

As we have seen, the widespread secularisation of society gave women equal treatment for the very first time in history. Attention was focussed on education, contraception and attempts to equalise the one-sided marriage contract. Yet, unarguably, we have more family breakdown, suicides, murders, violence, single parents, divorces and multiple marriages than at any time in history. Are women to blame for all this?

In other words, is the demise of religion and the consequent emancipation of women to blame for the breakdown of society and family values that we can see all around us?

In the past, women had no choice but to stay with their husbands even if they were abusive and alcoholic. This meant that there was a structure in which children were brought up but now, thanks to women being more independent, they can leave their husbands and bring children up on their own. I would never advise women to stay with an abusive husband but women have to see that many of the things which have happened because of secularisation and loss of values have harmed everybody.

The decline of religion has, as I see it, also brought about the loss of human and spiritual values. We have wars affecting more civilians than armed forces, a total breakdown of family life in many parts of the world, and financial greed such as never before. Over the past 100 years since religion stopped being a force in many people's lives, these things have happened. Whatever Dawkins, Hitchens and other detractors say about religion, this is unarguable.

Yet we will never bring back the power of traditional religions. They have gone forever and we need now to bring back genuine spirituality without the trappings and the male ego of old style religions.

Who will reawaken the world to spirituality?

It's got to be women at the forefront. Thanks largely to male-dominated religions, we have lost sight of feminine, or female, values. All the things we see as bad in the world such as wars, the financial meltdown, increase in violence and destruction of the planet through greed, have been brought about mainly by men. Yet in every case it is women and children who suffer most.

The breakdowns in our present society have happened because of decisions taken by men and it is now up to women to take the lead. We have thrown off the trappings of traditional religions and for all the historical reasons mentioned, women are now at the forefront. It has to be women who understand that there is an alternative way of living and begin the path that leads us back to God and spiritual values. This is necessarily going to be very different from the traditional religions which placed so many restrictions on women.

It seems to me that traditional religions cannot answer the questions people now have and nor, more importantly, can their adherents provide shining examples of the way to live a good life. They cannot show a mechanism from their own personal experience. Traditional religions, for instance, are often an incitement to violence because they all claim they are the only truth; yet they can't all be, especially if they say different things. If there is one truth, all religions must say the same thing.

As women have been so badly treated by men, why are women still sleeping with the enemy, as it were?

The problem is that even when given a choice, most people do not have the capacity to be self-sufficient. In the past, most women had no alternative but to marry a man, for sheer survival. The only exception was to be a nun in a religious order, and of course in the past many women took that option, or were walled up in nunneries, not always from their own choice but to save the expense of marrying them off to somebody.

Now, women do have the capacity to be self-sufficient and independent but most are not taking that choice. The idea that women have to be paired up is deeply embedded in society, and is continuing. It was maybe put there by religion, which weakened women's position in the world so that they had to depend on a man, but genuine spirituality can restore that independence of spirit which says: I am a complete person on my own.

As I see it, women can lead the way forward without religion but not without spirituality.

Chapter Two

Why and how women must lead the way

We have seen, in the previous chapter, that although men have shaped or interpreted religion for their own purposes, and all major religions, even nowadays, have a male at the head, women are naturally more spiritually-inclined than men.

In most Christian churches, the vast majority of worshippers will be female. And now, there are very many female vicars and ministers, in spite of Christianity being overall a patriarchal religion. Women have yet to penetrate into the hierarchy but I predict that before very long, we will have the first female Archbishop of Canterbury.

It's the same story on present-day retreats and spiritual gatherings, whether these are Christian, Buddhist or Hindu: around 90 per cent of the participants will be female.

Given that this is the case, perhaps it's now time for women to lead, rather than follow, and to bring the feminine principle to the fore. Briefly, the feminine principle – before we get on to any discussion of spirituality – is holistic, and seeks harmony and connectedness rather than separation.

The late quantum physicist David Bohm stated in his influential book, *Wholeness and the Implicate Order,* that the general tendency for individuals, nations, races, social groups and also men and women, to see each other as fundamentally different was a major source of conflict in the world.

It was his hope that one day people would come to recognize the essential interrelatedness of all things, and so build a more harmonious and holistic world.

This tendency for separation, to divide and rule, can be seen as the masculine principle at work. Throughout the ages, men have conquered and subdued, or attempted to, not just races, countries and women, but nature and the environment. The urge to conquer and overcome is at its most obvious in the military sphere, but in civilian life, the same expansionist, empire-building mentality is at work. We can see it in the way that once tiny companies such as McDonalds and Coca-Cola have become worldwide brands, all the while eating up smaller companies with ruthless takeover bids and asset stripping.

The concept of 'small is beautiful', although propounded by a man, the economist E.F. Schumacher, in 1973, seems to have got completely lost in the modern world whose motto has been, rather, the bigger the better. 'Too big to fail' has been a popular slogan of our times and yet, since 2007, we have seen how so many of these vast organizations, in banking, retail and manufacturing, *have* failed.

Few people would argue that it's men, or male values at least, that have come to the fore in our present society. And while this has resulted in many welcome advances such as the invention of anesthetics, electricity, cheap food and efficient methods of communication and transportation, there is a growing awareness at the same time that something is missing at the heart of things.

We, the present authors of this book, would define that 'something' as the female, or feminine, principle. The male principle has overreached itself to such an extent in our present society that we now have the potential, quite literally, for world destruction. Ever more countries are acquiring nuclear weapons and we have the very real threat of global financial meltdown as country after country once considered prosperous, reveals itself to be overwhelmed by unpayable debt.

The greed, dishonesty and risk-taking of the banking profession has only come to light in recent years and has shocked everybody to the core. Again, men have been at the forefront of these scams and malpractices. We now understand that there is no such thing as a 'trickle-down' effect, and that the huge profits that some banks have been able to make are not only at the expense of their customers, but that these profits stay firmly at the top, to fund the lavish lifestyles of the CEOs. A famous cartoon, published in the New Yorker in the 1940s, has a rich banker showing off his yachts in an expensive marina. His friend says: "And where are all the customers' yachts?" The vast fortunes of Arab dictators were revealed in the so-called Arab Spring of 2011, while much of the population lived at or below the poverty line.

The gap between rich and poor is increasing all the time. In the 1970s, in the West, the pay differential between entry-level workers and those at the top, thanks to union power, was not all that great. With the demise of the unions, it's not unusual for a CEO of a medium-size company to be on £1.5 million a year, while entry-level employees may be paid quite literally nothing. This greed at the top resulted in the many Occupy protests around the world in 2011, grass-roots campaigns that made many people sit up and think and start to reassess their values.

Money, greed, territorial ambitions, overweening profit motive – all these are examples of the worst excesses of the masculine principle at work. We have arrived at a situation where there are not many of the earth's finite resources left to plunder and where the concept of ever-upward 'growth' is being questioned by economists and environmentalists.

Some commentators believe that the masculine principle reached its worst excesses during the 1930s, the era of such dictators as Hitler, Mussolini and Stalin, whose activities have been well described.

Since those dark days, women have made enormous strides to even up the inequality they suffered for centuries.

But as yet, so Jayanti believes, not with a strong enough force or purpose.

Men have been brilliant at inventing things, from the washing machine to tube travel to aeroplanes to the internet to space travel and electricity. All of these have been wonderful advances and mightily benefitted many people in the world. Indeed, it has been said many times that the invention of the washing machine liberated more women than all the feminist tracts ever written and there is some truth in that.

Yet there is no moral imperative behind these inventions and technological advances. Neutral in themselves, they can be used equally for good or ill and in any case, may cause untold harm and (literally) man-made disasters, as the chemical explosions, oil spills and mining disasters of recent years have shown. Most of these happen when the profit motive has got out of control and there is not enough attention paid to the safety of the workers.

But at the same time as the masculine principle threatens to wear itself out, women have been coming to the fore in ever greater numbers. There are now more women than men training to be lawyers and doctors, and women are now creeping into the higher reaches of the judiciary and government. Indeed, German Chancellor Angela Merkel and head of the International Monetary Fund Christine Lagarde became known as the 'bail-out babes' as it was largely up to them to try and unravel the Eurozone crisis which became acute during 2011.

At the same time, education and contraception have meant that women can now take their place in the world, are able to earn their own living and be unburdened by having to have a child every year. More women than men, at least in America, are now taking higher degrees; for the first time in history, women are becoming better educated than men. The upshot of all this is that women have never had so much power and influence as they possess today.

So at this point in history, women are uniquely placed to come forward and lead the way into a future where the masculine and feminine principles blend in perfect harmony, and the restless inventive masculine mindset can be tempered with the more holistic, naturally spiritual inclinations of the feminine mindset. Women are uniquely placed to take charge, to assert themselves and to show the right way forward.

Jayanti, we have been talking about values, and how the feminine principle now has to take precedence. Does this mean you are now saying that men don't have values, or the right values? After all, it is still the case that men, not women, are spiritual leaders the world over.

Men do have values, of course, but at the present moment, it is the feminine values of love, care and compassion that are so much needed in the world today. The masculine values, of action, courage and pioneering were great and necessary when men were exploring the world, but nowadays we need to share rather than conquer and appropriate. Men need to develop the more feminine qualities but what I'm saying is that they come more easily to women.

In the past, masculine values have been given more importance but now it's time to bring the traditionally feminine values to the fore, as they are of more use in the world today.

There are hopeful signs. In the past, few men would have looked after young children but now men are taking time off work to be with their newborn babies. Until recently, the idea of paternity leave was laughed at but now it's common in the world of work. Also the word 'mothering' is giving way to the term 'parenting' and men are definitely taking a more active role in the upbringing of their children.

They now need to take these values into the wider world.

When do you think this was written and what do you have to say about it?

Woman's Nature Requires Obedience

We've had the impression that women as a class are more spiritually minded than men, with sensibilities more refined, and purer thoughts. Scriptures say the opposite is true! Women are more often led into spiritual error than men. Perhaps it is caused by her intuitive, emotional thinking. (Intuitive thinking is God's gift, not to be despised, but it needs the balance of a man's reason.) I should add too, that a woman does not have to be led into error. That is the reason God commanded her not to usurp authority over the man, so she can be protected from false doctrine.

Two hundred years ago?

It was actually written just a few years ago – and by a woman! This woman is a member of Quiverfull, or Christian Patriarchy, a newish American movement that says that women must be the helpmeets of their husbands, and obey them rather than trying to be equal or superior.

I'm astonished but I can explain it. The myth of patriarchy has always put across the idea of Eve tempting the man, and this has given a valid reason for men being superior. In Hindu scriptures it is considered that women don't have enough of an intellect to get to know God or to study the scriptures.

But what I would say is that there is no truth whatever in these ideas! Today, so many men are violent, alcoholic, abusive; why should we want to obey them? What gives men the right to imagine they are the ones who know everything? What sort of example are they setting?

It's often said that men are more rational than women but is this actually true?

I believe that God is now commanding women to use their spiritual qualities and inclinations to take the lead. Women have always had values but in the past, never had the courage to express them. They were always pushed down, belittled, never given equal education. Lack of courage is always connected with practical factors. If you don't have education, a profession, any money of your own or any way of earning any and keeping yourself, where is courage to come from?

And when you say that women must lead the way, how do you mean? There is much talk of 'positive discrimination' to get more women into the higher reaches of politics, law, medicine, multi-nationals. It is now the case, in the West at least, that there are more women than men reading subjects like law and medicine at university. Yet they are not getting to the top of their professions in the same way as the men. Are you arguing for positive discrimination to put more women in leadership positions?

I completely believe that we must have positive discrimination if women are to take their rightful place in the world of affairs. Equality simply won't happen by itself. Discrimination against women has been very active for centuries so now we must have positive discrimination to even up the score. For this reason, I am in favor of women-only lists for prospective MPs, for instance. In India, they now have such women-only lists and if they didn't give women the opportunity, it would never happen and there would not be any Indian women MPs.

We have seen in the previous chapter how religions, all over the world, have betrayed women and treated them as second-class citizens. There is no religion in the world that treats women as the equals of men. Perhaps we should start by defining the differences between religion and spirituality.

Religion can be defined as a set of scriptures, rituals and customs, whereas spirituality is the consciousness of an inner being and relationship with the Divine. Spirituality can be part of religion but is often lost when rituals take over and the inner core becomes lost. This is what I believe has happened to the major world religions today; the rituals have taken over and people have forgotten the essential message.

Although the present day militant atheism is often seen as a boys' club, ever more women are proclaiming themselves to be atheists, not wanting to be associated with traditional religions or the way they have put women down.

In the 1970s, feminists were very anti religion. This is what I discovered when I first began to attend conferences organized by the United Nations. This was because of chauvinism, and religion was intimately associated with the patriarchy those feminists were trying to pull down. Today, women are more receptive to spirituality and are recognizing that without some kind of inner experience there is emptiness.

So many people have not had proper information about the myths associated with religion, and have rejected it for that reason. For women, the patriarchal, hierarchical structure of traditional religions have made them want to reject all that religion stands for and we also have to take on board that society now allows you to be atheist. Atheists always make out they know more than you do and that if you believe in God, you don't have much intellect or brain power.

Atheism, for many, seems to indicate an intellectual capacity to think for yourself, whereas belief in God means you are taking on an antiquated and superstitious set of doctrines. And yet the vast majority of people in the world still do believe in God. Even if they no longer go to church, they believe there is something beyond the material and the physical.

Surely, since women have made so many gains thanks to secularization, to embrace spirituality would be a backward step?

I believe this to be an enlightened step, not a backward step. Spirituality will help us to achieve higher targets, to obtain clarity and calmness and to make balanced decisions. Spirituality will enable us to think straight.

Spirituality increases people's ability to get on with others, to work with them. It helps to clear the mind of unnecessary rubbish, helps to identify key factors when making decisions. In the world of work, a spiritual awareness helps people to excel, to get promotion and to be able to work in teams. In general, women work better in teams than men, and spirituality develops a team spirit. Team work is becoming ever more important in the world of work.

So how will we do it?

We will never do it by force or argument, only by example. We have to show and persuade people that the masculine principle of divide and rule has run its course and that it's time for a new beginning whereby the feminine principle will prevail.

We have to be able to show that the power of goodness is not just passive but an active force. The more we use the power of truth, the more we create an opportunity to move forward. When you serve people and win their hearts, you receive the return whereby they support you. If you adhere to the power of goodness and love in all your transactions, you will discover that people will support you.

In the past, it has only been intense campaigns and actual legislation that have changed anything, plus practical things like top-quality girls' schools being established. Surely just sitting and being spiritual isn't going to achieve anything?

Yes we need campaigns but for them to be successful nowadays they must be allied with a sense of spirituality.

So are we saying, at the end of all this, that men are evil and that women by contrast are wonderful?

Women can of course be just as greedy and materialistic as men. We see this in the consumer society, in shopping addiction and so on. Although the greedy bankers are mainly men and any notion of spirituality or accountability has been completely lost, women can get caught up in the shopping syndrome. Advertisers appeal to basic instincts and women buy into that. Women, I believe, are more susceptible than men to the power of advertising. For men, acquisition of money is the thing and for women, spending addiction.

Of course these are generalizations, but they have a lot of truth. There is a lot of truth in the current definition of a rich man as somebody who earns more money than his wife can spend.

But, one might ask, where does spirituality or a belief in God come in? Surely we can have a feminine principle without any belief in God or recourse to spirituality? After all, if the feminine principle is embedded within all, all we need to do is recognize it and it will come out, surely?

Although human beings have all the positive values inherent in them, it is only God's power that allows us to follow those values. In a world full of falsehood, it becomes difficult to follow the path of truth, and to bring values out and adhere to them.

If you just try to act as if God or spirituality exist, without really believing in the concepts, the danger is that values will keep disappearing. No human being is free from negativity and the vices of ego, anger, fear and worry. Such traits are deep within us and only God's power, as I believe, will enable negative qualities to be cleansed and erased.

Unless we retain some kind of belief in God and in God's power to remove negativity, we can so easily justify these traits. We can say, this is how I am, that I have a short fuse, am quick to anger, impatient, or whatever. Even people who sincerely believe in truth, honesty or justice but without recognizing God, will justify their anger or rage.

A misconception people often have about spirituality is that once you become spiritual, you will immediately become perfect. But it's not a static thing. Challenges will keep coming up and as you progress, you will discover all sorts of good and bad things about yourself. Spirituality is a process of peeling off layers to discover your true self. I often liken it to cleaning up a badly tarnished silver object. At first it's black, and a lot of black keeps coming off onto the cloth. But if you persist, clean it a bit at a time, eventually the shining silver object will emerge.

We are saying – or at least you are saying – that women must now lead the way if the world is to change for the better. Yet although there have been women's movements in the past, and women were instrumental in the phenomenal spread of early Christianity, it seems that men very soon took over and that none of these female-led movements lasted. Would you agree, and if so, why is this?

Women's movements have always failed in the past or been short-lived because of the ingrained belief, held by both men and women, that women are secondary to men. In Christianity, women were never given equal opportunities so any gains they made were always going to be short-lived. In social systems, women have never been given equal education, equal inheritance rights or equal power. Even today, women are still not getting equal pay or if they are, they are not given equal promotion. It is clear to me that men are never going to concede their superior status without a fight, so women have to claim it for themselves. For instance, it's still pretty much the case that if a child has to be taken to the dentist or the doctor, it will be the mother, and not the father, who has to take time out of work.

Although any adult could do this task, women are still the ones who look after the children and the household, even if they are holding down a full-time job. The typical male attitude is that his career is more important. Yet, for the first time in history, women can claim their power and exercise it.

We have seen, in that passage from the female member of the Christian Patriarchy movement, that this idea of women being secondary and inferior, keeps coming to the surface. This shows us that we have to be constantly vigilant. Women are still taking men's names on marriage, even though there is no longer any need to do so, and even though they may be higher earners or better educated than their men.

Patriarchy still exists in many parts of the world and we have a long way to go.

In the past, women traditionally turned to God from a position of weakness. The female early Christians were examples of this. God gave them strength. In fact, in its early days Christianity very much appealed to the weak and oppressed. In more recent times, the way that slaves adopted Christianity in America is another example of this; the negro spirituals, for instance, and fast formation of churches. Now for the first time in history, significant numbers of women are educated, independent, have their own finances and homes and also a voice. Would you say that women can now turn to spirituality from a position of strength?

Yes, absolutely. What spirituality can give us today is self-esteem and act as a stabilizing force to operate in the world with dignity. Men are now questioning their role in a world of change and without spirituality, you can get to the situation where men and women are at loggerheads and constantly arguing with each other.

How, exactly, will this strength manifest itself?

The only way is by internal transformation and dignity. The only way to lasting self-respect, as I see it, is through spirituality. If you base your self-respect on anything else, it can disappear. If you base your self-respect on looks, as women often do, these will disappear with age. If you base your self-respect on education, that too can fade away as you have to keep it up otherwise you quickly become deskilled. If you base your self-respect on your job or status, that too can disappear as you can lose your job. In fact you can lose anything – your status, home, job, money, family, health – everything except spirituality. It is the only thing that lasts. Every other skill or attribute can vanish or disappear.

As long ago as 1792 the early feminist Mary Wollstonecraft, in her book *A Vindication of the Rights of Woman*, said: "I do not wish women to have power over men, but power over themselves.' Would you say this still holds true?

I am amazed, not only that it was written so long ago but that I had never heard of this woman. Are there any statues to her anywhere? There should be. I completely agree with what she says and would add that spirituality gives us this power.

Note: for others who have never heard of her, Mary Wollstonecraft was a pioneer feminist. She had one child, Fanny, out of wedlock and then married the radical thinker William Godwin, with whom she had another child. Mary Wollstonecraft Godwin died in childbirth, aged only 38 and her daughter, Mary, married the poet Percy Bysshe Shelley at the age of 17, as his second wife. Mary Shelley was herself the author of Frankenstein, a far more famous work than anything her husband ever wrote. Shelley, it may be remembered, was sent down from Oxford for publishing a seditious pamphlet, The Necessity of Atheism. This was long before evolutionary theory, so maybe the arguments in favor of atheism are not all that new!

Why do so many people today resist spirituality?

People often feel nervous of spirituality because they are afraid it will isolate them and disempower them. They believe that if they take time to turn inwards instead of outwards, this will mean they take their eye off the ball and they will lose concentration at work, or on their other goals. But this is because people often don't understand the differences between religion, spirituality and superstition, which we have already addressed in this chapter.

Just to recap: *Religion* is above all, patriarchal. It doesn't answer questions but says we have to believe in the scriptures, and that in any case it's all a mystery. So many of the miracles, so-called, in Christianity, such as the Virgin Birth, the Assumption into Heaven, turning wine and bread into the body and blood of Christ, simply cannot happen scientifically. Yet Christians are asked to believe these things, even today.

Superstition, which includes new age and psychic phenomena, is also not logical and again, we are asked to believe. There are now psychic fairs being held in many countries, and people flock to them because they want to hear their future. But again, there is never a proper explanation of anything.

Genuine *spirituality*, by contrast, offers an explanation of things that simply cannot be explained on a physical basis, such as mind, personality, values, feelings, memories. On a very simple level, to accept the spiritual means that you take on board aspects of existence which are non-physical in themselves, but which affect the physical. For instance, you can go into a building, feel its atmosphere, and either shudder or feel relaxed and happy. The ambience of a place is beyond the physical yet it affects physical processes.

We've all experienced this. Yet can evil or goodness, as physical entities, be contained in bricks and mortar? In spirituality, we ask: how is it possible for the brain, which is physical, to create non-physical energy?

Spirituality happens when a woman realizes her own dignity, without fashion, make-up or external things to make her feel good.

So now women have to be spiritual?

Yes if we are to turn the world around and have any kind of future. Women are more likely than men to take the idea of spirituality on board as they are more used to dealing with the right side of the brain. The faith that women have had is always stronger than anything men have had. The transmitters of faith and spiritual knowledge have always been women. And that's why I say that women must now take the lead; it's too late to leave it to men. The reason is that feminine qualities are now needed more than ever. We need sustenance, compassion, nurture and kindness in the world, and only women can do that.

And yet all the great creative geniuses of the past, the painters, writers, architects, compilers of scripture, have always been men. Where do women fit into this?

As I see it, women have never had the time or opportunity to sit and reflect, to develop their creativity. For one thing, education is required to bring the intellect up to a level where it can do something creative, and until recently, women have been denied education. Then, women have been burdened down with children. If you start doing something creative, then every year or so you have another child, where do you find the time to be creative? In the past, almost the only women who achieved in a creative sphere were women without children. Great writers of the past such as George Eliot, the Brontes, George Eliot, Jane Austen, never had children. Also in the past, women were expected to relinquish any career or creative talent in order to bring up children. In Christianity, more or less the only women who achieved anything outside the domestic sphere were medieval nuns in convents. We have the opportunity to be powerful, yet even today I see women disempowering themselves.

How?

In order to realize your true qualities, you have to go beyond the consciousness of the body, and I see women becoming more body-conscious than ever. Women can no longer be themselves; they have to be 'groomed'. Just recently I was talking to a teacher who said that she was expected to be 'groomed' in the classroom, which meant, she had to wear make-up.

Yes, there was the case of a woman who worked at Harrods being dismissed for not wearing make-up to work. It is true that women – and men for that matter – are becoming more body-conscious than ever. Newspapers are full of how this or that celebrity has put on weight or lost it and there are endless articles about how good somebody looks at 40, 50, 60 and beyond. But isn't this also because it's now possible to keep looking young and healthy in a way that couldn't happen in the past? Isn't it part of the march of progress, in much the same way that mobile phones weren't around 20 years ago and anesthesia wasn't around 200 years ago? It's not morally wrong to want to look your best, is it?

No of course not; it is the expectations and the pressures that are wrong, and the idea that the outer, or physical, being, is the essence of *you*.

Do you think that the ever more lavish weddings of nowadays have anything to do with women disempowering themselves? They seem to be getting grander and more expensive all the time. One recent wedding in the newspapers cost £12 million, apparently.

Definitely. I believe that one major reason for the downfall of India is wedding competition. The modern Indian bride is expected to be educated, beautiful, groomed and also to bring a huge dowry to the match. The greed of the mother in law continues after the wedding and the bride's family has to go on providing goods such as cars, computers, motor bikes, whatever the husband's family demands. No wonder you have all these instances of a bride who does not come up to expectations being doused in petrol and in extreme cases, dousing herself as her life has become unlivable.

In the West, it hasn't reached this level but we have the

situation where women – and it is mainly women – will bankrupt themselves having a more lavish wedding than their friends and spending five-figure sums which would much more sensibly be spent on a deposit for a house or kept in the bank on deposit. Weddings are a huge waste of money and resources, and a potent way that women are holding themselves back. Weddings are an expensive kind of conformity, total selfishness, greed and unnecessary indulgence on the part of everybody.

They are strong words. What about children?

Again, here women have to take the lead. We all know that the world is currently in a dire state, that the earth cannot provide enough resources for everybody already on the planet, let alone more. This is not the time for self-indulgence or to ask: what do *I* want? We must ask ourselves instead: what does the world want – and it certainly doesn't want more people. Children have always been a very successful way that men have kept women down and the current state of crisis in the world is a war. When it's time for war, your priorities change and you cannot carry on as usual. Instead of giving birth to children, the focus of women has to be to try and change themselves, to concentrate on their own development.

But surely women want children? There is currently enormous emphasis on motherhood, fatherhood, parenthood and fertility treatments for people who can't have children. Also same-sex couples such as Elton John and his gay partner are now having children, so it's not just women.

In the past, women had little choice as to whether or not to have children. They were mainly the result of lust and ego on the part of the man, and women had very little option in the matter. In India, every woman had to be married; there was simply no alternative. In the West, there has been some tradition of spinsterhood but in many parts of the world there was not a choice for women to stay single. And until very recently, the vast majority of unmarried women were in the religious life, either in a community or teaching or nursing. Women have the opportunity for freedom now but they are not taking it. The reason they are not taking it is because they don't see a valid alternative. The alternative of remaining single, not having children, but devoting oneself to the greater good, has been lost.

Also, until very recently, most women in the West thought that they had to get married. It was a social imperative rather than a proper choice. Very few even considered not marrying or having children as the pressures were so great.

One reason women want children and relationships is because otherwise they fear they will be lonely and unloved.

This again is because they have not taken spirituality into account. With genuine spirituality, you are never lonely ... We have to take on board a completely new set of values, whereby a significant number of women are taking the lead, not in an aggressive or fighting way, but by example. When women see the example of some of the seniors in the Brahma Kumaris, they know they have got something special and not only that, we keep expanding, without any of us having conventional jobs or charging for events.

Would you say this is entirely because of spirituality?

There is no doubt of it. Because we spend so much time in meditation, in turning inwards, however busy the day, we can gain insights that are lost to people who are immersed in jobs, children, homes, social activities and so on.

What sort of insights?

The awareness of who you are as a unique being. This will not happen unless you take time to turn inwards and make it a daily discipline.

So we must stop indulging ourselves? The emphasis is that family life is the norm and something we must all aspire to. Even gay people are now copying heterosexual marriage and speaking of my wife or my husband, as the other half of a gay couple.

The message I have is very clear: we cannot indulge ourselves in every way. We simply don't have the resources. Apart from the question of how people conduct their private lives, there is the very serious matter of squandering resources and not paying attention to what is happening to the planet. For instance governments are reluctant to bring in austerity measures to reduce carbon emissions. That again is total selfishness. It has also been estimated by some economists that if everybody in America and Europe turned to a vegetarian diet, in 30 years we would be reforested. Yet the uptake of vegetarianism, world-wide, remains low.

The current state of the world is materialism., and we have forgotten or are denying the spirit. We have lost touch with values, which have nothing to do with matter or the material world. Love and peace exist in the human spirit. As I see it, women have an important role if – and only if – they are ready to acknowledge spirituality and bring these values into the world. Women have a major role in a global situation where there is loss of values. Fraud in banks is one aspect of loss of values, but there are instances everywhere. We have got to the stage where people believe that to rip each other off is clever.

I've read, in a book by Tim Parks called Medici Money, that although the Medicis were very wicked in the way they amassed great fortunes, on their deathbed, they repented of their sins and gave money back to be used for good causes because they were afraid they would go to Hell otherwise. They quite literally believed in Hell. Do you think that something has been lost because most people no longer believe in Hell – even though some like to believe in Heaven?

It's not so much a matter of heaven and hell as in cause and effect, or karma, which we will discuss in more detail later. If you believe that all deeds, good or bad, will rebound on you, then you are more likely to do good actions. This is a spiritual truth and one that women are more likely to take on board than men. But the old-fashioned notions of heaven and hell belong to the scriptures and no longer apply. If we want to secure a good future for ourselves, it has to be one where harmony and love apply in the here and now, never mind what might happen after death.

So now to sum up, can I ask again: why must women take the lead?

The feminine qualities are for harmony and love whereas the masculine ones are to divide and rule. When it comes to leadership, there has never been an instance of two men who have shared leadership. There is always one leader and perhaps a second in command, or the struggle for leadership has meant splitting into factions, or war and conflict. That is the male way.

But let's take an example of a woman-led organization, the Brahma Kumaris. When the movement began in the 1930s, the constitution stated that it would always be led by women. This was of course a very radical decision at the time, when no woman ran anything, at least not in India. Two women, both very young at the time, assumed leadership roles and they worked in harmony together for decades and never struggled for individual power. The Brahma Kumaris is the only organization in the world which caters for men and for women but which is administered by women who have led through the power of love. In our movement, nobody gives orders but everything is empowered by love. This is an outstanding example of how women can lead and we now need to bring these spiritual qualities to secular organizations, with women at the head.

The BKS grew from very small beginnings to a large influential worldwide organization. This shows it can be done by women and there has never been a coup or a power struggle.

I have to ask here: what will happen to men in this brave new world?

In a perfect world, men and women must have an equal role and that is what must happen, otherwise the severe problems of the world will continue and get much worse. Although men and women must be equal, this doesn't mean they have to be the same. Men have more of an affinity with left-brain thinking, which is logic, analysis, devising computer systems, engineering feats, inventing things and so on. Although women can do these things, they seem to come more naturally to men. Women tend to use the right brain more, and this is responsible for intuition, creativity and spirituality.

It seems to me that men in the past have hijacked everything: both logic and analysis and creativity and intuition. There has never been a female playwright to rival Shakespeare, perhaps the most intuitive of all dramatists, and there have never been any great female spiritual leaders in the past either. How can this change?

In spiritual understanding, or at least in Eastern spiritual understanding, the soul is neutral, and so the feminine qualities of compassion, love and intuition have to be balanced by the masculine qualities of courage, action and reason. Men and women have to develop both qualities so that the soul becomes perfectly balanced. Women now have to learn to deal with the negative feminine qualities of attachment, dependency and fear, and men have to deal with the negative masculine tendencies of ego, bossiness and anger.

When you say that the BKs lead by the power of love, what do you mean? What exactly is love, in this context?

Love means acceptance of other people as they are and the ability to give them respect and dignity. To love somebody in the proper sense means to inspire them to reveal their highest potential and help them deal with their own weaknesses. It is trust, an ability to radiate out to others so that you are never seen as a stranger, or hostile.

It means that even if you don't like somebody very much, you go beyond that and become able to see their good qualities. Love can also touch people with personality disorders such as schizophrenia, autism, bipolar disease, for instance, and help them to calm down.

When you embrace the power of love which is of course an aspect of spirituality and also a major tenet of Christianity, you become a role model for others so that when they see you in action, they will want to emulate you. When you learn to be in control of yourself, you don't want power over others, but have the aim to show the way to others so they can be as strong as you.

One accusation often leveled at female high achievers is that they pull the ladder up after themselves so that others cannot climb it. With the power of love, that cannot happen.

Chapter Three

Science and Religion

As religion has mainly been the province of men, so has science. What we call 'science' and the scientific method, which proceeded by demonstrable and repeatable evidence and proof, was developed by men in the nineteenth century, and until very recently, the vast majority of scientists were men.

Gradually, as science seemed able to explain many of life's mysteries, it began to replace traditional religion, which relied on magic, superstition, fear and myth rather than observable, quantifiable fact.

But for most of written history, religion has held sway over science, and on many occasions, whenever science challenged the accepted order set down by religion and the scriptures, its claims were ruthlessly suppressed by men of the church, sometimes by torture and death.

If religion tried to curtail the lives of women, it also did its very best to prevent scientific advances from being made generally known and often held that those who wanted to push forward the limits of knowledge and enquiry, were being Godless and wicked.

There is the famous example of Galileo asserting that the earth went round the sun instead of the other way round, but this is far from being an isolated case. Religious leaders have a long history of opposing advances in medical science and throwing in all sorts of moral and ethical objections to anything that may make life more comfortable and easy for people.

Thus 150 years ago they fervently opposed anaesthesia, especially for women in childbirth, as being against God's will, and they also opposed effective contraception, for the same reason. Men of God (so called) have also objected to safe, legal abortion, assisted suicide, assisted conception and just about anything else that may affect life and death. Jehovah's Witnesses, one may recall, continue to oppose blood transfusions, even where a patient's life is at stake.

In fact, one might say that almost every single scientific advance has been at some time opposed by one religion or another. Religions have also denounced radio, film and television as 'wicked', have been against air travel, central heating and anything that modernises or changes society. In fact, religion has until recent times exerted such a dead hand on progress it is a wonder that any scientific advances ever got off the ground.

In the past, the majority of people believed fervently in a God and understood Him to be the Creator of all things, heaven and earth, the planets, the solar system, the universe. In the West, the vast majority of people also quite literally believed in Heaven and Hell and in the concept of the eternal soul. The reward for good behaviour on earth was to go to Heaven and the punishment was to suffer eternal torment in Hell. The decision as to which place the dead would go was determined on the dreadful day of Judgment, and the prospect of being condemned to eternal damnation was held over the congregation by 'hellfire' preachers.

In addition, the Catholic church had the concept of limbo, where so-so souls could remain for a while as they worked their way up to Heaven. In most Western religions, it was popularly believed that we lived out just one bodily existence on earth and then spent an eternity as a soul, or spirit, in Heaven or Hell.

Eastern religions took on board the idea of reincarnation and karma, believing that our souls kept incarnating into different bodies or, at least until perfection was attained, when there would be no more rebirths and all karma was settled.

These, briefly, were the traditional mysteries attaching to the major religions. If they differed in many particulars, they all believed that humans – and in some cases animals and insects too – possessed a non-material soul or spirit which was, essentially, the most vital part of us and eternal and indestructible. The religions differed in what they considered happened to this eternal soul after physical death, and a huge body of literature has grown up around all major religions to try to explain the mystery, but all accepted without question the reality of the soul.

If not everybody could understand the mystery, they just assumed that the knowledge of God passed all understanding. Or, at least, it passed their understanding. Religion, as we have seen, infused every aspect of life in the past, and most of ordinary, everyday existence took place within the context of the prevailing religion of the country. Most people went to church, the temple, synagogue or mosque and even if they did not go regularly, they would be baptised, married and buried with the aid of the priest, imam or rabbi.

In the past, religion was intimately intertwined with the secular laws of the land; it still is, in many countries, so that ordained clergy have felt perfectly qualified to pronounce on such things as female dress, shops opening on the Sabbath, what people are permitted to read and what they should be allowed to watch.

But when it began to be possible to prove things by scientific methods and research, the whole validity and edifice of what was, essentially, scientifically unprovable, was called into question. Now, an increasing number of people began to ask awkward questions they had never dared to voice before, and for which in many cases religion had no satisfactory answers. If there was a Heaven, where was it? Where, or what, was the Soul? How could Hell exist? If Hell did exist, did an all-loving, all-forgiving God create a place of eternal damnation?

The concept of the Virgin Birth, a much-loved tenet of Christianity, took a dive when medical science discovered that any child born of a virgin and without the intervention of a man, would be an exact clone of the mother, and therefore female as there would be no male chromosomes. Gradually, it seemed that many religious beliefs were being disproved as a scientific impossibility. The idea that Jesus ascended bodily into Heaven after death, or that communion wine and bread could mysteriously transubstantiate into the body and blood of Christ, were shown to be so much nonsense as the march of science advanced.

Suddenly, or gradually, the concepts of Heaven, Hell and an all-avenging God began to lose their power to terrify, intimidate or exhort people into towing the line, and religion's long hold on the hearts and minds of the populace began to weaken. At least, the educated populace began to question religion's traditional tenets. We started to feel we had been hoodwinked by religion, and many of us living in a scientific age no longer wanted to have anything to do with a set of beliefs which asked us to accept nonsensical and impossible happenings as divine truth and wisdom.

Religion held sway for a time but it was like fingertips slipping off the cliff and in the end, science won – at least among the intelligentsia - until we have the situation nowadays where many people who consider themselves rational, logical and educated, would probably call themselves atheists.

Science seemed so much more modern and enlightened than the old-style superstitions and unprovable hypotheses associated with religion. Science was supremely concerned with evidence, with proof and with experiments that could be replicated time and again. There was a brave attempt to bring the two together in the nineteenth century, when science was gradually invading the universities as a proper subject for study, with the formation of the Society for Psychical Research, which attempted to bring scientific methods to bear on investigating paranormal phenomena.

If only science could prove the existence of the supernatural and the paranormal, it was thought, there need be no dichotomy between the two. The Society is still going, and has huge archives the public can consult on the reality of such phenomena as déjà vu, ghost sightings, communication with the dead and poltergeists, and the situation today is that there are certainly things which remain 'unexplained' by science, although definite proof remains hard to establish.

Finally, when Charles Darwin published his theory of evolution, and his hypotheses were gradually taken seriously and apparently hardened into proof, there seemed nowhere that God fitted in to the equation.

In the past, it was assumed that creation required a creator, and that God created heaven and earth and all that in there was. Then the theories of evolution appeared to negate this idea, as it seemed that living creatures evolved of their own accord, by natural selection. In his book *The Greatest Show on Earth*, Richard Dawkins (website slogan: 'a clear-thinking oasis') says that Charles Darwin's book *On the Origin of Species*, shook society to its core when it was first published in 1859.

The theory of evolution, put very simply, goes like this: Life on earth began about four billion years ago in the Hadean Ocean. Energetic forces driven by volcanic activity created conditions which allowed the formation of chains of molecules. Some became trapped within pores of solidifying volcanic rock which catalysed unusual chemical reactions. Occasionally a chance combination would create a new molecule capable of sustaining its own formation. Scientists say that ribonucleic acids are capable of this type of self-assembly today.

Eventually molecules called lipids, capable of forming cell membranes, would form. Then self-perpetuating chemical compounds could enter the forces of natural selection which would guide their ascent up the evolutionary tree to ever more complicated forms of life.

The controversy first set in motion by the publication of

Darwin's book, argues Dawkins, still rages 150 years later. Although evolution, according to Dawkins, is now accepted as fact by all reputable scientists and theologians, millions of people the world over awkwardly refuse to believe it and dare to question its veracity.

Dawkins asserts that although it is now possible to present a cast-iron case for evolution and all scientists can now point to living examples of natural selection in birds and insects, to 'time clocks' in trees, to radioactive dating, to fossil records and to confirmation of these notions from molecular biology and genetics, people are still not convinced about the truth of evolution, and the concept that we, as humans, have gradually evolved over millions of years from simple life forms or the primordial soup.

Not only that, says Dawkins but 'systematic opposition to the fact of evolution is flourishing as never before', particularly in America, where there are many 'insidious attempts to undermine the status of science.' The Christian Patriarchy movement, flourishing in some parts of America and Canada, believes in Young Earth Creationism, or YEC, and completely discounts evolution in favour of an Earth created by God relatively recently, certainly several thousand years ago rather than billions of years ago.

In his new book, according to his website, Dawkins provides unequivocal evidence that 'boldly and comprehensively rebuts such nonsense.' The problem with evolution, for the ordinary person who has not the time or education to go into such things, is the huge time scales involved. If changes happen over millions or billions of years, there is again no way that they can be conclusively proved, especially as there are no written records going back that far. In this way, much of evolutionary science depends on leaps of faith, as belief in religion or God does.

In fact research scientist Michael Barrett, professor of biochemical parasitology at the University of Glasgow, whose job consists of stripping life down to its chemical components, admits that divine interventionists could rightly argue that the chemical view of the origins of life is no more proven than the existence of their omnipotent creator.

However, Barrett goes on to say, in an article:

The unrelenting deconstruction of life's mysteries to their chemical bare bones leaves me believing that we really are no more than a bag of chemicals; our oldest ancestors no more than a string of self-assembling molecular building blocks; our very consciousness nothing more than the output of a chemically driven series of electrical impulses, selected ultimately, perhaps, to ensure the propagation of a seminal chemical reaction.

(New Scientist 6 April 2009)

Then something I would like to know is: why were dinosaur and other such fossils only found once the theory of evolution had been propounded? Why were they not around in Roman times, or Elizabethan times? Although there are many monsters and fabulous creatures found in myth and legend, these prehistoric creatures were actually supposed to exist. But, as with God, nobody has ever actually seen a dinosaur; unless you consider Jurassic Park to be a work of fact, not fiction.

There is a school of opinion which says that if you shout something loudly enough and often enough, people will start to believe you – especially if you howl down the opposition with emotive words so that it appears stupid, naïve and – the worst insult that can apparently be hurled at anybody these days – 'unscientific'.

However, by no means everybody is as convinced as Dawkins of the absolute authority of science and the scientific method. Theories of science themselves keep changing. The Newtonian model held that observable phenomena depend on the detached observer. The physical world, this model maintains, is not affected by the observation of the scientist, and what one scientist observes will be equally observed by another. This was the totally objective model which held that the physical world was determined and ran like clockwork of its own accord.

Then later came the highly complicated and still emerging discipline of quantum physics, which adheres to the idea of interaction, and maintains that the observer intimately affects the outcome of the experiment. But although science strives hard to be objective and beyond emotion, it is itself always changing. Nothing stays the same, even in theories, for very long.

The fantasy writer Terry Pratchett, whose best selling Discworld novels are all about fights between good and evil, between dark and light forces in the 'multiverse' has said: "Quantum physics is getting so weird the Angel Gabriel could turn up at any minute." Science is not one universal unchanging truth but at any one time, an interim statement of what seems to be the case at the time. Then, perhaps, more experiments, more findings, will change long-held suppositions.

Terry Eagleton is a tough-minded academic, not a scientist, but he has some equally tough things to say about science, and most especially science as Dawkins represents it. Science, argues Eagleton, contradicts itself all the time and that is what is known as scientific progress is very often anything but. In the past many scientific hypotheses which were accepted as unequivocal truth have crumbled to dust in the light of more evidence, more knowledge and different assumptions.

Every aspect of science, says Eagleton, starts off with an assumption, and in any case there are many things which exist or which are a reality, that cannot be demonstrated in the lab. Both free speech and imperial aggression, for example, undoubtedly exist, but we cannot prove them with any known scientific experiments, nor is this likely to happen at any time in the future.

Science, Terry Eagleton says, trades on certain articles of faith like any other form of knowledge, and these articles are liable to be overturned as new information comes to light. In any case, scientists have now reversed their formerly profoundly low status to become 'authoritarian custodians of absolute truth.'

Eagleton goes further, and writes that scientists are peddlers of a noxious ideology known as objectivity, 'a notion which tarts up their ideological prejudices in an acceptably disinterested guise.' He adds that science is shot through with prejudice and partisanship, ungrounded assumptions, unconscious biases and taken-for-granted truths. There are many telescopes, he asserts, up which science is reluctant to peer, and like the old-style religions, science now has its own high priests, sacred cows, revered scriptures, ideological exclusions and rituals for suppressing dissent.

Dawkins, Eagleton reminds us, is very tight-lipped about the cock-ups and catastrophes of science.

The situation now, broadly speaking, is that there are two schools of thought and of belief: the evolutionists, or Darwinists, who believe the irrefutable evidence is there to point to a very slow evolution of species; and those who uphold the idea of specific Creation, or as it is sometimes known these days, Intelligent Design.

The problem is that the evolutionists are usually better educated and in more prominent professional positions, than the Creationists. They are also more articulate and have more platforms to shout from. In this, they are rather like the orthodox medical practitioners and the alternative, or complementary practitioners. 'Science' can and does shout down the complementary practitioners from its great height, accusing them of quackery.

And yet, as anybody who ever has been very ill knows, there are serious limits to what medical science can achieve, especially for chronic conditions, and many people are genuinely helped by spiritual healing, aromatherapy, massage and art therapy, for instance, even though 'science' can never prove that these gentle treatments do any good. Dawkins has stated that there is no such thing as alternative medicine: 'medicine either works or it doesn't. ' But again, anybody who has suffered from a serious illness knows that this simply isn't true. A particular cancer treatment may enable one patient to 'beat' the disease, yet have no effect on another patient suffering the same type of cancer.

Then, very many medical treatments that have been tried and tested on animals in laboratories, fail to make the grade when tested on humans.

The novelist Tim Parks recently wrote a book, *Teach Us To Sit Still*, about how his long-time, debilitating back pain had been completely cured by meditation; a treatment impossible to test on laboratory animals. And there are many conditions which remain totally outside the reach of current medicine, such as tinnitus, multiple sclerosis, arthritis, Alzheimer's and other dementias.

Briefly the scientific position, as evinced by Richard Dawkins, who is, as Terry Eagleton said, the nearest thing to a professional atheist since Bertrand Russell, maintains that that the scriptural concept of an all-loving, all-merciful God is outdated and is, in any case, an instance of blind faith and superstition. The concept of God will not stand up to any rational analysis. As a Darwinist, Dawkins appears to believe that we are still evolving, but that it all happens so slowly that it is not noticed.

But if natural selection ensures that only the very best and most durable qualities will survive, we should be living in a world of peace, love, harmony, and plenty.

Yet we manifestly are not.

In his book *What God Wants*, author Neale Donald Walsch has this to say:

Asking the question as to whether humanity has improved since written records began, he answers himself:
..humanity still faces today the problems it has always faced.

And those problems have grown, moving in exactly the opposite direction *from that which one would expect of an evolving society. ... The problems of greed and avarice and abuse of power, the problems of poverty and hunger and disease, of the poor and the destitute, the hopeless and the helpless, the hungry and the starving, have not gone away. Those problems have increased, not decreased. ... The fact of the matter is that there is more suffering on the planet than a society that was truly civil would allow, permit or tolerate – much less create.*

Terry Eagleton has some strong words to say about Dawkins and the evolutionary, Godless approach he espouses in his own book, *Reason, Faith and Revolution.* Cleverer and wittier than Dawkins, Eagleton likens Dawkins talking about God to somebody holding forth on biology whose only knowledge of the subject is the Book of British Birds.

Dawkins, asserts Eagleton, has an old-fashioned notion of what constitutes evidence and seems to think there is no middle ground between things you can prove beyond all doubt, and what constitutes blind faith. In fact, says Eagleton, all the most interesting stuff goes on in neither of these places, and religion – specifically Christianity in Eagleton's case – was never meant to be an explanation of anything.

In any case, says Eagleton, science and theology are not talking about the same thing. If you have faith in somebody or something, this is not necessarily provable by a scientific method, but is a commitment to something you think might make a difference to your life.

To take a simple example: I may have faith that the horse on which I have bet some money will win the race. This faith is not something I can prove one way or the other, except by studying form and placing my bet. Other people may have equal faith that another horse will win the race and only the outcome will reveal whose faith was justified. But although the strength of my faith, or the other person's faith will not affect the result, unless we have faith we would not bother to place the bet in the first place.

Or to take another example of something we know exists but which cannot be proved by science: the power of love and attraction between humans. I may love you dearly, and in fact may be completely besotted by you. I may, as poets have done through the ages, extol your many virtues and wondrous qualities. Yet somebody else, while acknowledging that you have all these brilliant qualities, may not love you at all, or not even like you very much.

There is no scientific method in existence which can 'prove' that I love you, or that somebody else does not love you. True, our actions can indicate love or hate, and science can now show us which brain waves and chemical pathways are affected by the emotion popularly known as love. But science cannot come up with a reason as to why I may fall in love with person A, who others may consider quite unsuitable for me, but not with person B who on paper may be a much better prospect. The power of natural selection does not always provide the answer here, as the frequent breakdown of intimate relationships shows.

Although sociobiologists have argued, along Darwinian lines, that men choose women for their apparent fecundity and women choose men for their apparent ability to provide, history can show us literally millions of examples where this has not remotely happened. Desmond Morris made out an entertaining case for the mating rituals of the Naked Ape, in a best-selling book of the 1960s but the truth is that human love is far too capricious to be captured and explained by any evolutionary theory. Nor does it remotely follow animal mating rituals, although the imperatives of shelter, food and reproduction are similarly hard-wired in humans.

Eagleton goes on to say that the current idea that a religious view of the world has been put to flight by the steady accumulation of scientific evidence, that the Age of Faith has been heroically ousted by the Age of Reason, is simplistic and unhelpful. It was not, he asserts, that science gradually exposed the fallacies of myth and religion so much as that one moral outlook yielded to another and that scientific rationality represented a new form of human self-understanding.

Yet science and moral progress manifestly do not go hand in hand.

In his highly scholarly book *Atheist Delusions*, David Bentley Hart asks what good atheism has done, and answers himself by saying:

> *It is a strange presupposition that a truly secular society would be of its nature more tolerant and less prone to violence than any society shaped by faith. The modern age of secular government has got to be the most savage in history.*

Nature, adds Bentley Hart, has no moral principles at all.

Towards the end of 2011, a report, *Value and Values: Perceptions of Ethics in the City*, compiled by clerics at St Paul's Cathedral during the height of the Occupy protests, says that science and technology is largely responsible for the overweening greed exemplified by City workers. In his introduction to the report, Dr Giles Fraser, former Canon chancellor of St Pauls, wrote:

> *The fact that trading is now so heavily mediated by technology and less reliant on direct human contact may go some way to explain how a sense of moral obligation has come to feel less compelling.*

The relentless march of science and technology into all of our lives, and the atheism that seems to be part and parcel of it, are beginning to worry many people, who are asking where morals, ethics and values come from if there is no God, and if all religions are so much superstitious nonsense.

But many people now concerned at the apparent wide gap

these days between apparently rational, objective science on the one hand, and subjective, irrational belief on the other, are attempting to tie up science and religion and explain why so many of us continue to believe and to have religious-type experience which science cannot easily explain.

The new(ish) discipline of neurotheology, tries to tie the two together by closing an attempt to determine why ideas about God and a belief in the supernatural and the continuing existence of the human soul after death, persist in a scientific age. Much of neurotheology starts off with the assumption that the human mind needs to create God, rather than starting from the standpoint that God already exists and the human mind is attempting to know Him.

One of the first and best books on the subject, *The Mystical Mind*, subtitled *Probing the Biology of Religious Experience*, is a closely-argued, very even-handed and honest attempt by two academics to try and trace what happens to the brain during a religious experience and discover the purpose of the mystical experience. Whatever constitutes such an experience, there is no doubt that many people through the ages have experienced transcendental states. That is a fact that cannot be ignored by the most hardheaded scientific investigators.

The book asks: what makes something spiritual and why are religious experiences so powerful? In all theistic religions, God has been perceived as the ultimate reality, and the way this ultimate being is described has been remarkably similar in all traditions and cultures.

The authors question why this should be, and put forward the thesis that all religious phenomenology has arisen from neuropsychology. In many cases, the search for a God, or ultimate reality involves a ritual. Over time this becomes stereo-typed and repetitive and involves doing certain things in a rhythmic pattern. Meditation and prayer are the most popular methods of apparently communicating with a higher being.

Theology, say the authors, begins with a belief in a higher power; it takes this for granted and everything stems down from that. But can science shed any light on why humans should need to have this belief, or what positive benefits this belief might bring?

The book draws attention to the historic struggle between theologians and scientists as they are considered to be opposite and antagonistic to each other. But perhaps there are methods, suggest the authors – scientific methods – by which this immemorial gap can be closed. Religion does not attempt to represent objective reality in the way science does and so the systems are apparently mutually exclusive. In fact, they function in entirely different domains. The authors go along with Terry Eagleton in stating that there are some experiences and realities impenetrable by scientific analysis such as anxiety, trust, joy, love.

The relatively new discipline of brain science is concerned with understanding how the physical brain and the intangible mind interact with each other and although there is a long way to go, it is encouraging that work is now proceeding in these areas.

The state, or condition, of altered consciousness, at least in some adherents, is common to all religious believers and the mystical experience happens in both Eastern and Western religions. It can also happen to those who profess no belief at all in a God.

The mystical experience is usually defined as a mechanism whereby a human being can enter into the realm of God or the ultimate reality. In the US, according to a survey cited by the authors, at least 40% of citizens have had such an experience.

So what is it? The authors of *The Mystical Mind* define it as 'a numinous experience of the holy transformative experience of reorientation, courage and facing suffering and death. It is a strong experience of order and creativity in the world, and an experience of unity.

Meditation produces a powerful subjective experience of the integration of opposites.'

Like all experiences, these are interpreted and modulated by the human brain, a physical entity. During such experiences, the brain undergoes neuropsychological changes. The brain processes these experiences and they can be seen as electrical stimuli in brain circuits. The brain and mind either generates mystical states or allow us to experience mystical states, but in any case, a non-physical experience is sensed through physical activity of the brain.

When we have no other explanation, we develop myths in order to find solutions to mysteries. But science and the scientific method are themselves myths that help human beings to explain the universe.

As it is unlikely that human beings will ever know the cause of every little bit of reality, we will always generate Gods, powers or other entities to explain what we observe. We cannot do otherwise. Religious ritual, say the authors, aims at uniting opposites so as to achieve some form of control over a capricious universe.

The authors of *The Mystical Mind* take a broadly Darwinist approach and conclude that mystical and religious experiences are generated by the brain to help us to survive and try to make sense of our universe, not only in physical terms, but to try to order and unite feelings and sensations.

An article in the *New Scientist* in February 2009 attempts to explain why human brains need to create God. It starts off by saying that although many institutions collapsed during the Great Depression of 1929 (an era increasingly being compared with the credit crunch of 2007) one type of institution flourished as never before: the strictest, most fundamental churches.

Science, the article goes on, is now telling us why: it seems that human beings have a natural inclination towards religious belief during hard times. At these times, our brains conjure up an imaginary world of monsters, spirits and gods and the more insecure we feel, the easier it becomes to believe in these 'irrational' beings.

Some scientists now say that religion is itself an evolutionary adaptation that makes people more likely to survive and pass on their genes to the next generation. A shared religious belief therefore, helped our ancestors to form tightly knit groups that co- operated for survival. This theory maintains that religion was selected for by evolution, and gradually became a part of every society the world over.

Other theorists maintain that in evolutionary terms, the benefits of holding unfounded beliefs are questionable. A belief in life after death, according to anthropologist Scott Altran of the University of Michigan in Ann Arbor, is hardly compatible with surviving in the here-and-now, and yet all religions have this belief in everlasting life at their core.

Altran believes that religion emerges as a by-product of the way the human mind works, and that human brains create a tendency for supernatural thinking. It starts in childhood apparently and experiments with children have shown an innate capacity for believing in Gods, fairies and all kinds of supernatural beings, including having imaginary friends. In adulthood, we readily form relationships with fictional characters and celebrities we have never met. This, some scientists have argued, is a useful evolutionary skill as it enables us to form social hierarchies and anticipate what a common enemy might be planning.

Belief in some form of life apart from the purely temporary and physical is, according to certain scientists, the 'default' setting of the human brain, and is clearly seen in children and some primitive peoples, but education and experience later teach us to override it. Few adults believe in fairies, imps or monsters, at least in sophisticated societies, yet most children do.

The ability to conceive Gods, which some researchers maintain is wired into the human brain, was one aspect of creating religion but another, more serious aspect, according to some scientists, is our human sense of cause and effect, which enables us to see purpose and design in everything, even when it is not there. Again, there is a handy evolutionary explanation of this, which is that our wish to see cause and effect in everything is an inbuilt survival mechanism so that we will run away to avoid danger, even when we don't have to.

One simple example is, you hear bushes rustle, you assume something is hiding in them, so you run away in case.

Experiments with children have again shown that very young infants will readily see cause and effect, and imagine that everything has a specific purpose. Birds exist 'to make nice music', rivers exist so that boats have something to float on. When asked, children were also seven times more likely to say that plants and animals were made by God rather than made by people. Children tend to invent God without being told about God by adults, and our predisposition to believe in a supernatural world stays with us as we get older. Adults are also inclined to see intention and design where there is, in reality, none.

This does not mean that religious believers are necessarily childish or weak-minded, as they concentrate more on the moral implications of faith than supernatural attributes, but that a predilection for religion is an inescapable aspect of the wiring of our brains. It is part of brain circuitry, say scientists, and as such will never go away. Some experiments have also shown that professing atheists also attribute purpose and design to significant moments in their lives, as if some supernatural agency were intervening.

As such, in spite of Dawkins *et al*, atheists cannot completely deny God, but do their best to muzzle the religious tendencies within themselves as rationally, these do not seem to make sense.

The conclusion of this *New Scientist* article, by Michael Brooks, is that God will never go away and atheism will always be a hard sell. It is also never going to be easy to get to the bottom of the origins of religious belief.

At the end of the article, somebody added an online comment to the effect that if, as Richard Dawkins states, religion is propagated through indoctrination, and evolution predisposes children to swallow whatever their parents tell them (as obedience is essential for survival), where does this leave the 'innate' hypothesis? Dawkins suggests that evolved gullibility converts a child's predisposition to believe in God into a specific belief in the God the parents worship.

This article generated a huge amount of online comment, which just goes to show how controversial and unresolved the whole debate remains. There are many theories, many ideas, much mud-slinging and at the end of it, the basic question comes down to: are we still making progress?

In its simplest form, evolution assumes that progress is being made through the process of natural selection and the drive for survival.

By implication, this should mean that human beings, and life on our planet, are getting better and better all the time and that eventually we will arrive at perfection.

But is this the case?

Even the most hardline atheist evolutionary theorist would have to answer no. True, we have more sophisticated belief systems but have any of them decreased man's inhumanity to man – and particularly, to woman?

Science has, undoubtedly, given us many things for which we as a society are profoundly grateful. We have effective medicine and surgery, high-tech dentistry and in the main are living longer and healthier than ever before. We have clean water and sanitation in many parts of the world. We can contact somebody on the other side of the world in seconds, and it hardly costs anything. We can look up information on just about anything on the internet. Science has given us the internal combustion engine, jet travel, digital cameras and a host of extremely clever devices. And these devices are becoming cleverer all the time.

Although we hardly need more people, it is now possible to treat infertility by hi-tech means. Scientific methods of growing crops have meant that much of the world has plenty to eat all the time – too much, in some cases.

All this, it can be argued, is progress.

To sum up, Evolutionists basically believe that consciousness and all mental states arise out of matter. They believe there is no such thing as the supernatural, angels, life after death, God or gods, reincarnation or transfer of non physical energy from one being to another.

They believe that religion mainly arose out of the need of a community to stick together, and that ritual and worship binds a society together. Religion and myths existed before scientists came along with evidence and reason, so that now there is no more need to believe in God than in Mickey Mouse or Shrek — they are all non existent in reality

Time to bring in Jayanti·

Why do you think there is such a conflict nowadays between science and religion?

Hardcore scientists don't believe that there is anything more than the physical body. They believe that the mind is a physical entity in the same way as the brain. If I believe that I am only a body, this means that I have no control over my mind. By contrast, if I understand that I am a soul, this understanding is giving me power to discipline the mind.

Where there is only the material paradigm there is no accountability and conscience is dead. I say to Darwin and Darwinists: just look at the world we are living in. Even a bird keeps its nest clean. Even five years ago, people might have disagreed with this statement, saying that in general terms we were wealthier, more comfortable and better fed than ever before. Now nobody can dispute that the entire world is in dire crisis.

It seems to me that we are going to have to start rethinking quickly, as the results have come quickly and faster than anybody anticipated.

What do you think science has achieved?

On the positive side, there is more money, more technology, more information, more human resources. All these are the result of science and the scientific method entering our lives. On the minus side, there are more weapons, more children at risk, huge population increase and the destruction of the environment. These are also due to science.

For more than 60 years, the United Nations has been working intensely with all of these issues, yet in each of these areas the situation is worse than 60 years ago. The problems of the world cannot be changed by more science, but only when there is a change of consciousness and inside the human heart.

As long ago as 1968, the founder of our movement, Brahma Baba, was asking how we could relieve poverty, illness and food shortages. The short answers were that more money could solve poverty, medicine could overcome illness and food shortages could be overcome by donating more food. Ever since the end of the Second World War, immense resources have been poured into foreign aid, developing effective medicines and addressing food shortages. Yet not only have none of these problems been eliminated, they have got worse.

The cause of all these problems is anger, lust and greed and however much money or resources we throw at them, the problems will continue. Whether or not you adhere to a belief system, none of this can be denied. The stark fact is that in spite of the great advances of science, kindness has not increased anywhere on the planet.

The point is that where there is total secularism, there is no conscience. Instead, we lie and cheat all the time, believing there to be no comeback, and the proof of all this is the condition of the world.

We have seen the effects of financial meltdown worldwide, where there is no concern for pensions, for people losing their homes or for jobs and employment. It is all the result of greed and worldwide secularism. Although the financial meltdown cannot all be laid at the door of science, it is the association of science and progress with secularism which has brought about the present calamity.

There is total corruption everywhere and secularism and consumerism take people over further away from contentment and spirituality.

Compassion has gone out of everything. A few years ago, the British National Health Service ran a conference about returning to values. It emerged that there was so very much pressure on NHS workers that compassion, care and empathy were all disappearing from the health service. Family doctors now spend an average of seven minutes with each patient: what can you learn about them in that time?

How can Dawkins say that you can have compassion without God? Where is the compassion these days?

The late British campaigner Claire Rayner, president of the Patients' Association, said that nurses have become very cruel and inhumane. And she says that as a former nurse. Would you go along with that, that people in the caring professions no longer have a caring attitude?

It's not that they don't care. They enter these professions with every good intention, yet their idealism never lasts.

Since the advent of science and the scientific method, we have come to believe that everything can be proved, and that is one of the problems with God and spiritual things. Do you think the existence of God can ever be proved using a scientific method?

No, because you cannot give such a specific formula in the

spiritual dimension. Within the physical domain, if you follow a recipe you will create the dish, and by following the same recipe you can create the same dish time and again. Within the spiritual domain, this may not happen. I can tell you what meditation is and how to meditate but I cannot say whether or not you will have a transcendental experience every time, or whether you will have an experience today and not tomorrow, or tomorrow but not today. This is because meditation is a subjective experience which depends on a certain state of mind to be effective.

If your mind was a hundred per cent receptive all the time, then yes you could replicate the experience time and again, but in reality this doesn't happen.

With the phenomenon of spoon bending, where science and the supernatural meet, you may say, there is an explanation of how it can work. A spoon is a piece of metal which appears to be solid but actually the particles are moving and if you use the energy of the mind, you can shift the molecules. You do need to believe you can do it, but the fact is the molecules are shiftable.

Television sceptics believe they have comprehensively disproved psychic and supernatural phenomena by outing mediums and other such practitioners as their experiments virtually never hold up when exposed to the harsh glare of television and also, sceptical observers.

When cameras are focusing, there is a lot of distraction and the vibrations of cynicism will adversely affect the outcome, as well. This is the old paradigm of here's the observer and here's the object. We know now enough about science and particle physics to be aware that the attitude of the observer can have an effect on the outcome.

What do you think can never be proved or demonstrated by the scientific method?

There is a vast range of human experiences which can never be proved in a lab simply because they are so specific to individuals. When it comes to falling in love, I may fall in love with somebody who leaves you cold. Fear is a similarly subjective emotion. I may be very afraid of something about which you have no fear. For instance, I may be very nervous of flying but you have no such fears; I may be frightened of spiders, but you cannot understand this fear.

Grief is another, very strong emotion which is specific to individuals. When a loved one dies, you may be consumed with grief or you may not; very often you don't know how you will feel in advance of the event.

There is little that science can tell us about the origins or purpose of these emotions because they are not universally felt about the same thing. Some people have never felt love for another, some people have never felt fear and others have never felt grief. Some people are tender-hearted whereas others are much more hard hearted.

Do you think that the advent of science has had any benefit on religion?

Undoubtedly. The priestly caste in all religions held sway until science came in, and one of the great advantages of science is that it threw out superstition. Science attacked superstition and dealt it a body blow. In the past, religion meant adherence to rituals, blind faith, superstition and obedience without under-standing. As I see it, all these things have gone or at least they have lost their power, and it is now time to offer true spirituality to people.

Do you feel that there are spiritual laws which are just as inexorable as scientific laws?

Yes I do. If we accept that scientific laws govern the physical world, and that they are very certain, we should also take on board that spiritual laws, which are just as exact, govern the world of thoughts, feelings, emotions, accountability and regard for others. If we remember this, then we will have accorded each discipline its rightful place.

Just to remind us, what are the spiritual laws?

Only if I have the right words, thoughts and actions can I achieve happiness. The original attributes of the soul, or spirit, are peace, love, truth, purity and joy. If I use these in my life and share them with others then I will prosper and allow others to benefit. If I go against these, I will hurt myself and others. The situation today is that instead of peace there is violence; instead of love there is hatred; instead of truth, there is falsehood; instead of purity there is negativity and instead of happiness there is pain.

Spiritual laws say that we must have respect for the self, for other people, for the dignity of life, respect for all forms of life as all forms of life are connected.

These laws are as inexorable as the physical laws which govern the material world.

The poet Coleridge once wrote, of the book of Genesis: 'And then man became a living soul'. Do you think that materialism and science can ever explain those words?

No.

Does this mean that the great poets know something the scientists don't?

Undoubtedly, which is why their poetry has lasted through the ages, and in many cases means just as much to people now as it did hundreds of years ago; the poets have been speaking truth.

Chapter Four

I want a better world: where do I start?

One does not have to be an old-fashioned preacher, gushing out threats of fire and brimstone and eternal damnation for the wicked to know that our present world is far from being a happy, peaceful place.

The main religions, supposedly dedicated to bringing about peace on earth and goodwill to all men (and women of course although that is never said) have manifestly failed us. We do not remotely have peace on earth. Religion's representatives have let us down either by preaching outdated and inappropriate doctrines, or by absenting themselves from involvement on the world stage.

Almost the only active religionists these days are the fundamentalists who are trying to put the clock back by insisting on repressive, outdated and often cruel and barbarous practices. Whatever God may want, he certainly doesn't want cruelty, torture, terrorism, suicide bombers and unsolvable and bloody schisms.

Religion has not worked and yet, as we have seen, secularisation has not worked either. Science is also not answering many of the questions we have on morals, ethics, compassion and kindness; where they come from, why they are important or why they might matter.

It is true that increasing secularisation in the world has done away with some of the more ridiculous trappings of religion, but at the same time, our present Godless attitudes have brought us to the brink of destruction and despair. The idea that all of life is some Darwinian survival and that humans are kind, honest and compassionate towards each other because that way we survive better, may be a nice idea but it is certainly not happening in practice. In fact, it often seems as though the best way to survive in the world today is to be as greedy, dishonest and exploitative as possible. And if there seems no accountability or comeback from wicked actions, where is the incentive to act honourably and decently?

It appears that neither secularisation nor a return to old-style religions will achieve the positive results that are needed to make the world a better place, so we will have to take on board an entirely new way of looking at things.

The new ingredient in the equation is that before we ever start thinking about reforming society, giving to the poor or campaigning against injustices, we must begin by examining ourselves and getting to know ourselves. It is the only way. Never mind anybody else for the moment, we have to look at our own ingrained and maybe negative attitudes and work towards self-improvement before we can hope to reform anything or anybody else. .

This may sound easy, yet for so many people, looking inwards is the most nerve-racking and frightening journey of all. For this reason, few of us do it, but before ever asking whether God exists or whether his existence can be proved or demonstrated, looking inward must happen.

The famous 12 steps of Alcoholics Anonymous and the related 'anonymous' organisations ask addicts to take a long, hard look at themselves and make sure they forgive everybody around them, rather than looking for others to blame. It is well known in the addiction world that addicts are liable to blame everybody but themselves for their problem. The saying, 'It was a woman who drove me to drink'– sums up the prevailing attitude which is that, in the addict's mind, it is always another person, or external circumstances, which has brought about the addiction, never themselves. Something or somebody else is always to blame. This process has come to be known as denial.

It has also long been understood in the world of addiction and recovery that nothing can happen until addicts take total responsibility for themselves and stop blaming others for their plight.

Nowadays, we first have to understand that we are all addicts. Although we may not be addicted to an actual substance, we have all become addicted to negative states of mind. They have become so ingrained that we often come to think of them as an integral part of our being. We say that we are angry, have a short fuse, have a temper, are depressed or impatient, for example, and tell ourselves and others: that's just the way I am.

In fact, such states of mind are acquired habits and the first step on any spiritual path is to address them and see what can be done to remove or reverse them. And even though we have said in this book that women must lead the way to spirituality, of course the advice and information given here is equally applicable to men!

The only way to start making ourselves better people and bring out the good qualities within us, says Jayanti, is to make time to sit in silence. When we go inwards and allow ourselves to be alone with our thoughts, we will gradually learn how to separate the positive from the negative.

This is how it is done, but like anything worthwhile, it does take practice.

This chapter continues and deepens the ideas first introduced in Chapter Two, and further develops the argument that women have to take the lead in transforming the world. Yet before this can happen, it is vital to work on the self and for that, Jayanti believes, we need to enter regularly, the world of silence and self-reflection.

When I try to turn inwards, what should I focus my mind on, right at the start?

You have to begin with the understanding that you are a

spirit, that you are a soul and that this is your body. I can't prove that there is a soul and nor can anybody else, but you can try this exercise: ask yourself, who is speaking, and what are the things which are clearly non-physical but which are definite qualities?

The answers will come quickly. They are: the memory, the personality, feelings, emotions, conscience, love, trust, honesty, altruism. None of these qualities is physical in that you cannot weigh them, look at them, see them or hold them. They all transcend space and time and you can recall an emotion that you had yesterday, or 30 years ago. You can also project any of these emotions and feelings way into the future but you cannot show them on any instrument.

You can, however, show results. Because of the existence of the microchip we know that a vast amount of information can be stored in a tiny space, so it is not a huge leap of the imagination to suppose that these qualities may also be stored in a tiny space or perhaps no space at all.

If that concept is a leap too far, start off with a hypothesis, as they do in science, and take on board the supposition that you MAY have a soul. Think of the soul as software and the brain as hardware. The brain is the instrument through which all this non-physical functioning happens. If something affects the hardware, the software is always affected as well.

When you begin to understand that the essential qualities which make up the individual known as you, and that these are separate from the body, it then becomes possible to focus attention on this non-physical entity which is at the core of your being. After a time, you will start to feel the energy of the personality and begin to be aware of the soul as something separate. But this will never happen unless you begin by sitting in silence. This is the essence of what meditation is, and it enables you to get to know yourself.

Do you promise that this will happen, that I will start to become aware of 'myself' as separate from the body?

Yes, definitely. You will gain the awareness that it is the attributes beyond the body which make us all unique, and that this uniqueness is something beyond gender, race, height, age or position in the world. When you sit in silence you can start to see where the mind is going and whether it can remain still or whether it is racing about all over the place. You will gradually come to the understanding that the mind is going over and over the past like a broken record and is out of control.

Then gradually, through taking time to sitting in silence and meditation, you will become aware that you are the creator of your own thoughts and can start to take charge of them. If you believe you are only a body, only an agglomeration of compounds and molecules, you believe you have no control over your mind and thoughts. Something external makes you angry, something external makes you upset or miserable, and without this silent time, you believe you have no control over your emotions, thoughts and mental habits.

But by contrast, once there is the understanding of the presence of the soul, you gain power to discipline the mind. The mind is like a horse and in the same way as you have to break in a horse, you have to tame the mind by first befriending it. Then you can train the mind and it starts to obey you, again, like a well-trained horse. This gives you the choice as to whether you go in the direction of a rough or an easy ride.

We suffer from anxiety, depression and worry because we don't know we are souls and that we can, if we choose, rein in these emotions. We also have to understand that we are always our own worst enemies.

But once the mind is kept in check, we start to realise we have choices in life we never realised we had before. We have to understand that the qualities which have brought the world to its present condition are anger, lust and greed. Everybody has to accept this, whether or not they adhere to a belief system. The problems of the world can only be changed when there is a change of consciousness within the human heart.

Where there is a world of secularism there is no conscience. We lie and cheat all the time and the proof of this is the condition of the world.

Do you think women have less commitment than men to the current status quo?

The old way of life never offered women very much so it is easier for women to think about a different *modus operandi*. The danger with a secular lifestyle is that if women start to ape men they will suffer from the same problems. At one time, women were less prone than men to cardiac conditions but as they live an increasingly masculine lifestyle, they are catching up. Women's cancers are also on the rise, and these illnesses are indicative of the stress that many women are under these days.

In the past, many women had no choice but to be housewives but now it is expected that women will both have a job and bring up a family. And increasingly, women are having to do this as single parents as well.

The breakdowns in society have happened because of decisions taken by men so the solution cannot come from that quarter. Women are now, for the first time in history, at the forefront of change and nowadays, have the education and the independence to start the process. It is mainly women who understand that there has to be an alternative way of living and begin the path that leads us back to God and spiritual values.

These values are going to be very different from the traditional religions which placed so many restrictions on women.

Traditional religions cannot provide the solution to the problems we now face, they cannot provide good examples or show a mechanism for a personal, life-changing experience. Traditional religions can be an incitement to violence and they all claim that they hold the only truth, yet they can't all do this because they say such different things, and claim that God wants different things.

How are women going to lead the way back to spirituality?

The most important aspect, before anything else, is to have the understanding of who you are. First of all and vitally, you have to let go of the consciousness of being female, young, old, white, black, a mother, student, career woman, grandmother, wife, housewife as these are all just roles that you play, some of them only for a short time. They are not you. If you identify too closely with your role, then you may feel bereft when that role comes to an end. For instance, some people may feel they no longer have a sense of purpose when they retire, as they have regarded themselves as a doctor, lawyer, engineer or whatever. A woman who defines herself through her children may suffer the empty nest syndrome when they leave home.

The main problem with identifying too closely with a temporary role you play is that you never really find out who you are separately from that role. Our social culture divides people into identities that are not based on a spiritual identity which is timeless and beyond all these temporary positions.

Once you come back to your spiritual identity you start getting in touch with your own inner world. When you do this and sit in contemplation or meditation, after a time you will find something stirring within you, something moving within you. After a time, you will discover that the world out there is not satisfying you and makes you feel empty inside, rather than full of love and happiness.

It has been found that when people win huge sums of money on the lottery, they imagine this sudden windfall is going to bring them everlasting happiness and then discover that they are exactly the same as before. A sudden huge cash injection into people's lives never delivers more happiness and stability, even though people often imagine it will. Also think of all the problems that can be caused by inheriting a large sum of money; so often it is squandered and not used to any good purpose. A spiritual law says that money without effort is wrong, but we have lost sight of this.

It is imperative that we start to separate ourselves from the external world, in order to see things as they really are.

Many of us have enjoyed what we consider the good things of life – enough money, a nice home, plenty of food, a social life, friends and family, a rewarding and fulfilling job. We have accepted that women's present state of equality and independence throughout much of the world has been due to secularism rather than religion. Are we in danger of turning the clock back, going back to repression, if we turn our back on the material gains we have achieved?

Yes there have been many gains and it is true that organised, traditional religions held women back for centuries. But we also have to understand that every time an action is repeated it creates a habit. This eventually becomes so strong that instead of having a choice, we have become addicted instead. At a very simple level this can be seen with cigarette smoking, which starts as a definite choice, maybe looks cool at first, and then rapidly becomes an addiction over which we have no control. All types of drug addiction, eating disorders, self-harming and relationship addiction are examples of actions which, by being repeated endlessly, have turned us into addicts. You then get to the point where the only important thing in life is to feed the addiction, and at that stage, everything which is most valuable in life has disappeared.

Many women nowadays suffer from anorexia or obesity and both are major problems in the world today. They are different sides of the same coin and come from feelings of inferiority and anger, where there is no love for the self. Low self esteem is very common these days.

We are increasingly living an unnatural lifestyle where so many people never take exercise, eat only junk food and listen to junk music, films and television. Men are part of all this as well of course, but women have a greater capacity to start turning things around and are more able to start moving on a spiritual path. At our retreats, the proportion of women to men is always at least 75%, which indicates that women are more open-minded about spirituality and more ready to consider something different.

What I am saying is that although in many ways we may seem to be materially comfortable and prosperous, all of us have got into a condition whereby genuine choices have been lost. It is only by going into silence, spending time alone with the self, that addictions can start to be separated from genuine choice, and real values can come to the fore.

Won't spending time with ourselves make us lonely?

We have become frightened and nervous of being alone and try to fill up every moment with noise. People turn music on the minute they get into their cars, the minute they get back home after work. We have become so drawn to external stimuli that we don't know what to do in silence. Many people can't bear even a minute of silence so they will break it by phoning somebody, even for mindless chatter. But when people learn that there is a way to tap into inner joy, it is actually impossible to be lonely.

The situation for so many people today is that they feel lonely when alone but when they are with other people they feel hemmed in.

Women are natural organisers but at times like Christmas, they can't cope. Helplines such as the Samaritans are always busiest over Christmas as women feel boxed in by their relatives and start arguing. Yet the prospect of spending Christmas alone makes them feel more lonely than ever; it's as if everybody in the world apart from them is having a merry time. The spirit nowadays is so deflated and bankrupt that we can't cope either with other people or on our own. But once we begin to love the self, we can be happy and cope with either situation.

You say that women have to lead the way back to spirituality. Yet it seems to me that what most women still want is a life partner, home, children and a career, with the life partner at the top of the list. We have so far in this book identified men as the enemy, the people who have, throughout history, marginalised and denigrated women and not accorded them equal status. So why do most of us still want to find Mr Right, and is this compatible with embarking on a spiritual quest?

Most of us do not have the capacity to be self-sufficient and so we look for somebody to lean on. In arranged marriages, there is exactly the same idea, that you are not strong enough to cope on your own but need somebody else to 'complete' you or to infuse you with the strength you don't have yourself. But the reality is that you multiply two halves and become a quarter. You actually become more depleted with somebody than when you are alone, but people believe they need another person in their lives. Nowadays, few women want to enter into a state of bondage or to make vows, but they do want a partner.

For many women there is not a free choice as to whether to be alone or in a partnership. So often women become attached to dependency and this means they are unable to make a free choice.

I am always reminded of the story of Erin Pizzey, the first person to set up refuges for abused women. It was 1985 and Erin was being given an award at the Strand Hotel. There was a huge demonstration in the street outside and banners saying: Down with Erin; Erin has Betrayed Women. Erin had been writing about how women behaved when they left the refuge and saying that within 12 to 18 months of leaving they would have found another abusive partner. She understood how this addiction to abuse worked, and meant that the women were permanent victims. The feminist movement at the time couldn't see the truth or wisdom behind this statement, that there was a pattern of abusive addictive behaviour which meant they kept repeating the cycle of abuse and could not get out of it.

It is certainly the case that dating sites, for both men and women, are now among the most viewed in the world. But are you saying that the quest for a life partner is an expression of weakness on the part of women – and men come to that?

The fact that so many people go through a lot of partners in their lifetime and it is no longer unusual to have three or more marriages, speaks for itself. We look for a life partner, a Mr or Miss Right, but mainly we don't find that person. If you look at the condition of the planet, you will see that the last thing we need is more children. Yet everybody wants a child of their own.

In many societies, grandparents put pressure to have children. They say: when are you going to give me grand-children? Yet they are not usually willing to take part in the upbringing of these children. The idea of new life, new blood, is deeply programmed within us but more of us must start to question the whole idea of reproduction if the present rate of population growth, the population increasing by 80 million every year; that's 150 new people born every minute. There's an old saying: there's one born every minute, but the planet can no longer support the amount of people born every minute.

We are all in a state of dependency, and feel that we need help by forming an alliance with another person. But mostly, this arises out of weakness rather than strength.

Although women tend to be more open-minded than men and are more willing to try new things, it is also the case that women have deeper attachments to men than men have to women. Their dependencies are stronger, possibly more deeply embedded and that is why it is still easier for a man to have an affair than a woman.

But if women decide to adopt a spiritual response to things, all the old power struggles between the sexes will stop in an instant. It seems to me that women are more prone to anxiety than men because they haven't been able to take charge of their lives. Where there is insecurity, people are attacked by doubt and women in particular are likely to put themselves further into bondage when they feel helpless.

The way out of bondage for women is always: education. It is the way out of the trap of poverty, dependency and feeling trapped. Spiritual education is also a major factor in liberation. When somebody is empowered with knowledge, they are enabled to break the shackles and take risks. Yet you need courage and you cannot gain this courage without meditation and the clarity of knowledge. It is not possible to move forward without a clear understanding of who you are and what you want to do.

Do I have to believe in God to start thinking and behaving in a spiritual way?

No. The way to start is firstly to accept responsibility for the self. It is critical to get to know yourself before you can think about God. Women are often told, and indeed brought up, to put others before themselves. But putting yourself first is not selfishness, just essential. It entails getting to know yourself as you really are and this is not a matter of ego, but it means you start from a position of strength.

Secondly, it is essential to make time for spiritual study. This means finding some courses, some spiritual meetings, retreats and weekends that you feel comfortable with. There are many such organisations these days and so much information on the internet that there will almost always be something suitable near you.

There are just three cautions I would raise:

Firstly, if an organisation is truly spiritual, it won't charge a thing. Sunshine, air and rain are free so why should spiritual knowledge be charged for? These days, many so-called gurus are charging very large sums of money for courses which go way beyond the need to cover costs for food, accommodation, literature and so on. For these people, God and Mammon come together but what sort of price can you put on imparting genuine spiritual understanding?

Secondly, the organisation should not focus on a charismatic human personality. It is the wrong way round that spiritual movements should have at their head some personality around whom a personality cult develops.

Thirdly, if anybody in the movement tells you not to ask questions, don't go with it. A truly open spiritual organisation should welcome any questions that the seeker has to ask.

What next?

The key to becoming spiritual is to give it time and attention, as with any other form of study. So the next step is to give oneself time for silence and wake up before you normally would in order to sit in silence. This takes practice but it gets you going on a spiritual path. But it must be done every single day and not just when you have time and when you feel like it.

I go to the gym every single morning at seven am. At first it was very hard to motivate myself to do this but now I feel I've missed something valuable in my life if I don't go. I feel slobbish and lazy. Does the same process happen with dedicated spiritual study?

Yes, it's exactly the same. The very first step towards acquiring spiritual knowledge and proficiency is to get to know your own inner being. Usually, for most of us, attention is always focused on the outside, on other people, and never on ourselves. We never give ourselves time to get to know the most important person in our lives: ourselves.

Also if you give time to inculcating a good habit, in time it will drive out the bad habits. But as the bad habits have so often become ingrained, they won't vanish of their own accord.

What will happen as spiritual study progresses?

Gradually, your outlook will start to change. When you start working on yourself you create an inner state of responsibility and accountability. One of the most important lessons to learn is that you can never change anybody else, only yourself. One major problem with women is that they are hooked on complaining. But gradually, a different consciousness will become apparent, as you pay attention to your own qualities and stop dwelling so much on other people's bad habits and negative states of mind.

Can you tell me what happens in meditation?

When you start meditating, the first thing that happens is that you find out about yourself. That is why so many people are nervous of it – they worry about what they might discover. You have to practise having awareness of a soul being detached from the body and use the mind to have the right type of thoughts. Here, meditation commentaries may be helpful as they give people an idea of what sort of thoughts to have. It's important not to blank the thoughts out, not to have a mantra or an image but to use thoughts to let the mind think about the soul. Thoughts create feeling, and after a time there will be an awareness of the separation of body and soul. This will lead to the ability to get to your original qualities. Without this information and regular practise, these qualities won't come to the fore.

But once you can connect with these qualities, self esteem and dignity will return. Once there is true value for the self, this will automatically be reflected in behaviour towards the self and towards others. You will become less discriminatory, less judgmental and more able to see everybody else as distinct human beings.

In many parts of the world there is racial hatred and we don't realise that this discrimination is caused by lack of self-esteem on the part of the haters. Where this happens, we don't see people from other races as distinct human beings, just as an undifferentiated mass.

Can you have good feelings towards yourself and others without meditation?

It's not easy because of all the negative qualities that have overridden the good ones. The only way to have positive emotions and to keep hold of them is through meditation. Otherwise, although good feelings may come, they are likely to be temporary.

For a hundred years or so now, scientists and psychologists have studied negative emotions. They are easy to study as they have a big impact, and the results of anger, depression, lust and greed are also plain to see. Positive emotions have only been studied systematically since about the mid 1980s and research is rapidly coming to the conclusion that only meditation can make positive emotions last.

It has become quite exact; if you meditate every day for a month, the benefit will last two to three months. Gradually, you will become aware of the following:

That I the Soul am the driver of the vehicle which is my body;
The Soul is the actor on the stage and allows interaction with a wider perspective
My home is my temple and I am now becoming aware how I feed it. Soul consciousness teaches you how to look after the body.

So meditation definitely does something?

Yes, it's not just airy-fairy New Age nonsense but enables you to change and improve your perspective on all sorts of issues as well as reduce stress, anxiety and tension within the body. But much more than that, meditation puts you intimately in touch with the core of your being.

Do you think that by sitting in contemplation and meditation, we will start to be able to separate right from wrong, to become aware of the things we should be doing and able to solve moral dilemmas by ourselves?

Yes I do. One of the qualities that will emerge through meditation is that of compassion. Compassion is where you care for another and it is one of the golden rules of traditional religions. But you have to separate compassion from attachment and this is often difficult for women. Attachment is where there is a need for love and you want to take, and when it doesn't come there is pain. Where there is love, there is the ability to give. Attachment is negative, whereas compassion is positive. We have completely lost sight of right and wrong, and this is because we are no longer connecting with the innate qualities within ourselves.

In today's world parents spoil their children and call it love. Yet overparenting is a real problem in the world today.

Can you give a couple of practical examples of where compassion should be separated from attachment?

Yes. Suppose my spouse has embezzled funds and the case comes to court. He, or maybe she, asks me to perjure myself so that he will get off and not be found guilty. Should I do this? My answer would be no. The right thing to do in this case is to reassure your spouse that you love him but you say it is only going to lead to more trouble if I perjure myself in court.

Or to take another common scenario: your son is on drugs and keeps pestering you for money to feed his habit. He threatens to kill himself if he doesn't get the money. Should you give in? You have to say to him, while in my house you follow my rules, and if you don't want to follow my rules, which include no drug taking, you will have to get out.

There was a famous British case about just this, where the parents turned the teenage son out of the house for being a junkie. The son kept slinking back to the house when he ran out of money and his parents even paid a couple of months' rent on a flat for him, but he continued taking drugs, none of his jobs lasted long, and he soon ran out of money to pay rent on the flat. His mother, a well-known author, wrote a book about it. Do you think she did the right thing?

Definitely, especially after giving him a chance. Compassion means the ability to think about the future consequences of your actions. In this case, the son would keep skulking back home for food, shelter and money while he knew he would always get it. I'm not so sure about broadcasting it to the world in the form of a book, though.

Should we then always follow the law of the land? Is this part of doing right actions?

Yes, you have to follow the laws of the land in which you are living. This is part of the responsibility which comes from being on a spiritual path. If you choose to have a television, for instance, you should pay the TV licence whether or not you agree with this method of funding. It's exactly the same with taxing and insuring your car. These rules are there for a reason and must be obeyed. If you believe that a particular law is wrong or unjust then you should campaign against it. But you cannot live in a country and not abide by its rules and still be spiritual.

Will these practices lead to an awareness of God?

Yes but it is essential to get to know the self first. Many religious paths say just the opposite, that having an awareness of God will lead people to do the right thing. My own understanding is that we must take it the other way round, and become conscious of what the mind and emotions are doing before we can hope to connect to God in any meaningful way.

Would you say women find it easier than men to meditate?

Initially, I would say it's about the same for men and women. When it's a new skill to be learned, both men and women find meditation difficult. Many will give up at this stage as they find their thoughts wandering and they get bored with sitting in silence. But once the practice of meditation is established, it seems easier for women to surrender their consciousness and receive God's love, which we will define and explain later.

Culturally, women have always surrendered to their husbands, never the other way round and the image of God as the bridegroom crops up in all religions.

What if I can't seem to meditate?

A lot of people believe that meditation is all about having an amazing experience of light, bliss, super-awareness. But this will not happen for everybody. For most, it is a gradual process of learning to focus thoughts on the awareness of having an inner being and appreciating core positive values. If you are having these thoughts, then you are meditating and anything beyond that is a gift.

Look at it this way: if I spend time thinking about you and understanding you better, I'm not wasting my time. If I spend time reflecting on God, I come to know and understand God better, and that is meditation. If I start to feel a connection, that is what we call yoga but even if I don't experience that connection, I am not wasting my time. We can all meditate up to a point and for all the process of meditation is beneficial. On the strictly practical level, research into meditation has shown that it can decrease blood pressure, relieve stress and tension and ease the symptoms of many illnesses from migraine to irritable bowel syndrome and digestive disorders.

Are all meditation systems equally beneficial?

Nowadays there are many different meditation systems and not all acknowledge the power of God. All systems are beneficial as they give value to a quiet time but not all systems will help people to get to know themselves better. Not all help people to connect with their inner self and to be fair, not all of them claim to.

But we all need help with meditation. We need clear guidance, and a teacher. Meditation is not something you can just pick up from time to time. It takes firm intention and regular practice, just like going to the gym, learning a new language, or any other discipline. You have to give regular time to meditation and push through the bad times as well as the good, as there will be struggles and times where you feel you are not getting anywhere.

A note on meditation:

Meditation is at once the most ancient and most modern of spiritual and self-awareness practices. All religions have a form of meditation, contemplation or prayer which adherents are required to practise regularly. For thousands of years, meditation was intimately tied up with religious practices, but from the 1950s it has had a secular application as well.

In all religions, meditation is designed to enable people to connect with their spiritual essence, the essential aspect of themselves. But it was not until the latter half of the last century that meditation was studied scientifically. To date, over a thousand medical and scientific studies have been carried out, and all studies report considerable health

97

benefits from regular meditation. It seems that sitting quietly and turning inwards brings about profound changes in the neurological process, and can reduce stress, depression, headaches, many kinds of pain, hypertension and have a positive effect on both emotional and physical health.

Some studies have also reported that meditation increases alertness and concentration, and enables the intellect to achieve new insights and understandings. The exact mechanism by which all these benefits are attained, remains unclear or, at least, it has so far not been identified by medical science.

But it does require regular practice, and many people are impatient. Although some doctors nowadays may recommend meditation for patients suffering from hypertension or other stress-related conditions, the usual response is, 'give me the pills, doctor!' Taking pills seems easier than setting aside time for regular meditation.

The usual recommended time to achieve benefits from meditation is 20 minutes in the morning and 20 minutes in the evening. In order to find time for this, many spiritual organisations advise getting up early in the morning. Indeed the Brahma Kumaris start their meditation at four in the morning, a time of day known as 'amrit vela' or the early hours of nectar. Monks and nuns also rise early for meditation or prayer. Then there is more meditation throughout the day, always at very set times.

At BK centres, early morning group meditation is practised, in total silence, with eyes open. During the day, meditation times are often accompanied by music or taped commentaries. They also have the practice of 'traffic control' where, at certain times throughout the day, you stop what you are doing and go into silence for two minutes. This, they say, enables you to be aware of the heavy mental traffic going through the mind, and to still it so that stress and tension do not build up.

There is no physical or hatha yoga practised at BK centres; it is all stillness, peace and sitting in silence or with very quiet music.

Meditation is also an aspect of some forms of physical yoga teaching.

The word 'yoga' actually means to connect, and the physical postures, which go back thousands of years, were originally designed to enable religious devotees to conquer the body in order to become aware of the mind. In modern practice, yoga is usually a secular form of exercises, usually with some quiet time at the end of the session, although it is not always associated with a religious or spiritual journey these days.

There is no possible harm that can result from regular meditation practice. Some people find they go instantly into a blissful, transcendental state but this does not happen with everybody. As with anything else in life, it is harder for some people to do than others, but there is always benefit from these quiet times. Although meditation can be practised alone, its effect is strengthened when doing it in a group.

A personal addition from Liz: I first became aware of the dramatic effects of meditation by proxy. My then husband and myself were both working at the Daily Mail, my husband as medical correspondent. His job was extremely pressurised and stressful and although he was a young man in his thirties, he began suffering from high blood pressure. One day, on impulse, he went to Westminster Abbey where the Dalai Lama was speaking. After the talk, there was a meditation session; at the time, this was a completely new concept to my atheist husband.

Greatly to his surprise, he had the most blissful otherworldly experience of peace, light and peace, and this led him to becoming a regular meditator. Before long, his blood pressure had returned to normal, where it has stayed. This was over 30 years ago, but for him the benefits have been so great that he has continued his daily meditation practice ever since.

In the following chapter, we will discuss how regular meditation can enable an awareness of God, or a higher power, to be realised.

Chapter five

How do I come to know God?

We explained in the last chapter how, by regular meditation, we can get to know ourselves and gradually, be brought to an awareness of God, whoever or whatever he or she may be. By meditating, taking time out of our busy lives to sit in silence, we will gradually be brought to an awareness of the things of the spirit, and which go beyond the physical.

Perhaps a useful analogy at this point would be with the process of getting to know another human being. When we first meet somebody, it is their physical presence which strikes; what they look like, what clothes they are wearing, the color of their hair, their height, race, their physical shape, whether or not they are wearing glasses, and other distinguishing physical features.

Then as we get to know them better, we will become less aware of their physical characteristics as their personality starts to take over. Mostly, the connection stays at this level, but in some cases and with some people, we can go deeper and experience becoming connected with their innermost being, their non-physical aspect.

This is the experience of meeting a soulmate, and when you are connecting with that human being, it is something that transcends time, space, place and also personality. It is a connection of spirits, spirit to spirit, heart to heart, and it is a connection that poets in love have often described.

Those who have experienced this connection know that there is a strong chemistry that goes beyond molecules or anything measurable that can be shown up on a scientific instrument. It is an electricity and a vibration, an involuntary connection. We know that we can connect with this person in our minds at any time and indeed, with the strongest connections of this type, they are always in our minds. We are always thinking about them and, most likely they are always thinking about us.

It is this kind of sensation that can come with the connection to God, and has perhaps been best described by the English metaphysical poet John Donne, who first wrote about the souls, hearts, minds (and bodies) of two humans intimately connecting with each other and then, later, wrote equally passionately about connection with God in, often, strongly sexual language:

> Divorce me, untie, or betake that knot againe
> Take mee to you, imprison mee, for I
> Except you enthrall me, never shall be free
> Nor ever chaste except thou ravish me.

With humans, the strong connection with another person often felt at the beginning of a love affair, does not always last but through regular meditation, a steady connection with God can be invoked and maintained at any time. It is, says Jayanti, a gradual process which becomes stronger the more it is practiced.

Jayanti, can you explain for us in a little more detail how connecting with the inner self can lead to an awareness of God, or a sense that there is something beyond us which is out there somewhere?

After practicing meditation for some time – and don't forget that as with any learned discipline there may be stops and starts and times when you feel that you are not making any progress – you will begin to be able to connect with your inner being at will. As this happens you will be able to feel that you are a being of light and peace.

When meditating, everybody will eventually experience this whether or not they believe in God. And then, for most people, comes the awareness that they are connecting with somebody or something outside themselves. The spiritual aspect of themselves will start to connect with something that seems bigger, more universal than they are and it often happens to their great surprise.

But I don't believe it can happen without first getting into the regular habit of meditation.

So you can have an atheist meditator?

Yes, and here is a true story that illustrates what can happen when you get into the habit of regular meditation. Some years ago a confirmed atheist came to us wanting to learn meditation. He had an enquiring mind and loved the concept, the idea of God but could not take on board the kind of God spoken about in the traditional religions. For nine years, he meditated regularly with the BKs at our morning sessions while remaining an atheist and then one day, he told us that he could suddenly feel the presence of God.

He'd had a bitter divorce and told us that even before he started to believe in God, regular meditation had allowed him to have civilized encounters with his former wife. This happened purely because he took the step of connecting with himself, and that allowed him to experience the peace and tranquility that he was able to take into his dealings with others.

So there is hope for the Dawkinses of this world?

I'm not saying that every militant or confirmed atheist will eventually experience a connection with God, but if they give themselves the opportunity to connect with the best aspects of themselves, yes, they could end up as believers.

But the first step must always be to connect with the self?

Yes, otherwise one might just have an intellectual appreciation of God that does not bring about any personal transformation of character and outlook. There are many people who would call themselves religious, or believers, and yet are full of anger, fear, worry and every type of negativity. The really important aspect about connecting with the non-physical aspect is self-transformation. My belief is that this cannot come about by an effort of will; only by regular meditation.

So first of all, start to meditate, make it a feature of your daily life as this is the absolute foundation to receive the love and wisdom that can only come from God. The more somebody practices the awareness of connecting with their peaceful, loving inner being, the more it stays with them and becomes a feature of their everyday life and experience. The limitations of physical identity fade away and with time, comes the sensation of another energy being reached and flooding in. But you have to open yourself up to it; it won't happen otherwise.

But we have to go beyond the physical?

That's right. It is the only way of coming to know God. We can read all the religious and spiritual texts, go to church, synagogue or mosque but unless we meditate as well, this other energy will not reach us.

If my nose is blocked, I can't smell the fragrance of roses. If I am firmly locked into physical and bodily consciousness, I will only believe what I see and feel with my five senses. But if, by contrast, I allow myself to go beyond the physical senses I make it possible for God's revelations to reach me. It's a bit like a radio receiver. If I have not tuned into the correct frequency, I will not be able to hear the music or other programmes being transmitted. The reality is that the waves, the vibrations, were actually there all the time and the more I am able to fine-tune my receiver, the more messages I will receive. And I will come to understand the messages and hear what God wants me to do.

But as so many atheist writers have pointed out, throughout the ages, many people have professed to hear the word of God

and in His name, have committed terrible atrocities. I think it is this kind of behavior, often accompanied by unbelievable cruelty, such as burning people at the stake, which has turned modern society away from God and away from religion.

Yes that is true but those people have always wanted power over others. Unless you sense that your whole being is flooding with light, peace and love, you are not actually connecting with God. Anything which gives rise to bad behavior cannot come from a true connection. The people who committed terrible atrocities in the name of God may have been perfectly sincere in their belief that they were wiping out evil, but if they perpetrated more evil in so doing, they were not acting from a genuine connection with God.

As BKs, we believe that it is only now, at this time of history when the world has got to a state of evil and corruption which cannot be rectified by governments, environmentalists or economists, that God truly reveals himself.

Today, our minds are mainly tuned towards the physical. Yet when we begin to tune to the inner world, we open up ourselves to the possibility of receiving what God is transmitting.

Can you explain in everyday language what sensations we will experience when we connect with God? I know that mystics and poets have described such a connection in the past, but it's often in language that's difficult to penetrate.

I will try. When you connect with another human being you know that the individual is there, a separate entity from yourself. This happens whether you are meeting personally, or connecting via email, telephone or any other means. You know that the person with whom you are connecting is not you. However close you may be, however much love you have for that person, you are still aware of another entity being present. It happens even with mothers and newborn babies. There is a very strong connection and bond and yet the mother knows that the baby is a separate being with its own personality, from the very moment of birth. In a similar way, when God's vibrations are reaching you, you know that there is a person or entity out there that is separate and different from you. God is not part of you, but another being. The major difference is that God does not have a body but is pure spirit and energy, and this is what scientists and atheists find difficult or impossible to appreciate.

In the past, it has been mainly poets, mystics and other highly sensitive, educated individuals who have been able to feel this connection. Now, the ordinary person can learn a method of going inside as well, and be able to do this at will. A person who meditates can do it at any time they choose and this way they will come to know God. It is the way all mystics have used and it is not exclusive to one religion or one type of person. I am describing a method by which anybody at all can come to know God if they so choose; no intermediary is required.

There is so much illusion and wrong thinking about God and many people who believe also think that God is unknowable, a mystery beyond human understanding. What I'm saying is that the revelations God makes plain are open to everybody and they will be the same for everybody. They are identical to every human being and are not restricted or expanded by study, by research, by any particular religious path or background.

You speak of meditation as being the way we will get to know ourselves and, eventually, God. But many people have had transcendental experiences through mind-altering drugs, such as LSD. There have been many books written about altering consciousness through drugs, and poets, artists, musicians and other creative people have often used them to arrive at an experience which has then been relayed to others. We think of Coleridge writing Kubla Khan under the influence of opium, and I'm told that a dramatic experience of happiness and positivity can be brought about with cocaine. What is the

difference between taking a mind-altering drug and meditating? Surely the drug can act in a fast way without going through the laborious process of meditation?

There have also been many other ways that people have induced a state of altered consciousness, such as fasting, whirling Dervish-type dances, magic mushrooms. It seems that humans have always had a desire to induce altered states of experience. What is the difference between these and meditation? Some people even believe they have seen God while under the influence of a psychoactive drug. What's so special about meditation?

Yes, you can get there with drugs or by taking extreme risks such as climbing Everest and many people have, both past and present. But drugs are addictive and have adverse side effects. Most other ways by which altered states of mind can be induced are also dangerous. You can induce a meditative state with drugs but there are serious downsides, none of which happen with the practice of meditation.

Through meditation, which costs nothing and does not lead the person into an illegal or addictive way of life, you come to experience a sense of purification. You come to know that the source of all this love, power, joy, compassion and profound peace is a point of light you can connect with at any time. There is no need to seek out a dealer or shell out lots of money for the experience!

Once a person becomes aware of this information, connection with God is only ever one thought away. It becomes easy and also, reliable. But it has to be individual. We are talking about a personal connection with God and you don't need anybody else to make it happen.

If connection with God is so easy, why do so few people seem able to connect?

Mainly, because they haven't had this clear information. They have been confused about what or who God is, what God does – concepts we will explore further in the next chapters - and they have often imagined that one needs complicated ritual and dogma or the intermediary of a priest, rabbi, imam or other professional religious leader, to come to know God. It has never been made clear to people whether God is within, without, part of ourselves or something separate, whether God is everywhere, in every tree and flower, whether he intervenes in human actions, whether he is the creator and destroyer or what.

It is difficult to connect when you don't know what you are supposed to be connecting with.

Are women ideally placed to make this connection?

Yes because women are less wedded than men to the externals. Women can be more independent of structures and formalities. As we are talking about what is essentially a journey of the mind, it's not necessary to have a church or specific place of worship. You can have a meditation corner in the smallest home.

And yet women are now becoming ordained ministers, priests and rabbis in unprecedented numbers. When I was a child, there was no such thing as a female Anglican vicar. Now there are probably more women than men being ordained and becoming country vicars at least, even if the higher echelons have so far eluded them. Would you say this is happening because traditional religions are losing their power?

Yes, definitely. But having said that, it is the case that an opening has now been provided, and that women at last have a foothold in the major religions, from where they can begin to make a difference. Traditional religions will change as ever more women enter their ranks.

Finally for this chapter, what happens when an individual is able to make this connection with God? On a practical level, I mean?

Once you are able to connect, everything in your life becomes clearer and more ordered. This will include every practical aspect of life including finances, relationships, your house, your job and your health. Now, you won't want to be horribly in debt, you won't want a messy untidy house, you won't want to have bad relationships with others, and you won't want to stay in a job that is no longer fulfilling and satisfying. Once you come to know God, everything will improve because God shows the way.

Chapter Six

Who or what is God?

At this point in history, there are two dramatically opposing views about the origins of life. One is the evolutionary explanation, which has the blessing of mainstream science behind it and into which has gone much scientific research. This was discussed at length in Chapter Two, and is pretty much accepted these days by all educated, non-fundamentalist people. It has become orthodoxy, replacing the previous orthodoxy which maintained that God created everything in seven days.

The science of evolution is still evolving, we might say, and many fine brains all over the world are currently trying to establish the existence or otherwise of the so-called sub-atomic 'God particle'; an elusive substance which, if found, will explain how matter comes about and is transformed into other kinds of matter (to put it simply).

If discovered, this particle will have nothing to do with God, in spite of its name. It belongs to quantum physics and not to theology, and will shed no light on whether or not God exists.

The other explanation of how life began owes nothing to science. This is the Creationist idea, otherwise known as Intelligent Design, which states that God created the world according to the book of Genesis, and that the Genesis account is literally true. Needless to say, this theory is widely decried and shouted down by most educated people of today.

It is held sacred by certain fundamental groups such as the Jehovah's Witnesses and Seventh-Day Adventists – who hold their Sabbath day on a Saturday, just to be awkward - but finds no credence in the scientific world or even by many religious believers.

For somebody like myself, neither a scientist nor religious adherent but a seeker, both theories raise unanswerable questions. To the evolutionists, I would say: if everything happened by chance, what is the point of anything? Where is the accountability? Also, when there are such huge time scales involved, how can we have irrefutable evidence of how many billions of years ago things happened, especially when written records go back no further than about 3000 years?

Not only that, but a question physicists have been tussling with recently is: how can something be created out of nothing? An editorial in the New Scientist magazine in January 2012 asked: How do you get a universe, complete with the laws of physics, out of nothing?

Perhaps this is where theology and cutting-edge physics try to meet, but there is no satisfactory answer. Scientist Lawrence Krauss, author of *A Universe from Nothing: Why there is something rather than nothing*, believes that the universe is most likely powered by 'nothing' and that we really can have something from nothing, that our universe arose from its existence within a multiverse, and all the universes have their own laws. Our own universe, he concludes, is just as it is for no particular reason.

The book has an afterword by Richard Dawkins, who says this book is cosmology's deadliest blow to supernaturalism.

But does evolutionary theory mean that we have to discount thousands of years of theology and divine teachings, all the beautiful buildings, poems, music, schools, universities and hospitals, dedicated to the glory of God? In the city of Oxford, where I live, there is a beautiful religious building every few yards and for the past 800 years, the university has been a hotbed of religious ferment and debate, occupying some of the finest minds of the time.

Very many of the colleges have Christian names – Trinity, Christchurch, St John's, Jesus, St Anne's, St Hugh's, All Souls, for example. Most of the older colleges have wonderful chapels which at the very least, are popular tourist attractions for visitors from all over the world.

So is this entire city, founded as a Christian seat of learning, built on so much nonsense? Richard Dawkins, who also lives in Oxford and who has benefited greatly from his tenure as an Oxford don, would appear to think so.

And to the creationists, I would say: if God created everything, then who or what created God? The creationists hold that the Earth, the solar system and the entire universe were created in a much shorter time than the Darwinists maintain and that one species did not evolve out of another. Perhaps seven days is pushing it, but they tend to believe literally in the Book of Genesis, and they discount evolutionary science.

If God created everything, did he also create evil? Is He responsible for everything that happens in the world, bad as well as good?

I, like many others, cannot believe that there is no guiding principle of love, goodness and benevolence in the world, that every impulse is somehow encoded in genes, yet nor can I believe that God created our entire intricate universe and presides over everything we do as some almighty judge.

Luckily, there is another explanation that, although unfamiliar to many, at least answers many vexing questions and provides an explanation of the otherwise inexplicable.

This explanation, which is probably more ancient than the Book of Genesis and certainly older than science, holds that time is circular, rather than linear. It is a concept familiar enough to Eastern religions such as Hinduism and Buddhism and is intimately connected with the doctrine of karma, which we will explore in the next chapter.

According to this concept, there are four major time cycles and these endlessly repeat themselves throughout all eternity.

First comes The Golden Age, where everything is perfect and there are no wars or any kind of strife. In Middle Eastern religions, this time is remembered as the Garden of Eden. After this comes the Silver Age, where things become slightly more tarnished. Then we enter the Copper Age, where things go from bad to worse. Finally, there is the Iron Age – our own time - characterized by greed, violence and the loss of all spiritual values. By this time, God has been pretty much forgotten or at least, completely discounted.

The eternal cycle understood by Eastern religions can be seen as a kind of evolution in reverse. Instead of the Ascent of Man, we have by contrast the Descent of Man. In this doctrine, Man becomes ever more degraded as time goes on, rather than more elevated.

. When things can get no worse, according to this belief system, God intervenes to usher in another Golden Age and the whole cycle starts again. Only God, outside of all this, is unchanging.

Nonsense? Well, it has a strong echo in classical literature, and we get a glimpse of the concept in the famous poem by John Milton, *On the Morning of Christ's Nativity*. This astonishing virtuoso work, written by the young poet at the age of 21, brings a Christian interpretation to the eternally repeating cycle beloved of Platonists. The infant Jesus will usher in a new era of peace, light and goodness by putting to flight all the false Gods, and all the evil and injustice in the world. Jesus' reign on earth will mean that:

Time will run back, and fetch the age of gold,
And speckled Vanity
Will sicken soon and die,
And leprous Sin will melt from earthly mould;
And Hell itself will pass away,
And leave her dolorous mansions to the peering day.

Yea Truth and Justice then
Will down return to men,

Orbed in a rainbow; and, like glories wearing,
Mercy will sit between,
Throned in celestial sheen,
With radiant feet the tissued clouds down steering;
And Heav'n, as at some festival,
Will open wide the gates of her high palace hall.

With the benefit of hindsight, we know that this did not happen
– or has not happened yet - and although Christ founded a major
new religion, we did not return to the Age of Gold. Instead, we
have inexorably progressed to the Iron Age, its exact opposite.
Whatever we choose to call our present age, nobody could call it
Golden. Indeed, the writer G.K. Chesterton said that the golden
age only comes to men when they have forgotten gold.

It could be argued that the ancient notions of both circular
time and the creationist story in Genesis are products of a pre-
scientific age and that now we are much more logical and
sensible. God has been rationalised out of the equation.

But supposing, just supposing, that we have followed the
advice given in the previous chapters about meditation and now
have an awareness of God, or to put it in more modern language,
a sense of love, power, goodness, compassion, that seems to
come from outside ourselves.

What kind of being, or source, are we talking about? The
educated, sceptical man or woman of today is not likely to accept
a patriarchal God, a God of vengeance, or a God who pronounces
women inferior to men; a concept that the great John Milton held
dear when, in *Paradise Lost*, he writes that Eve was 'not equal, as
her sex not equal seemed', in relation to Adam. And although
Milton sought to 'justify the ways of God to man', his
pronouncements, if not the poetry, would not find much favour
with the emancipated, equal woman of today.

Most modern women are not even going to take on board the
idea of a male God, or the three in one idea of an all-male Trinity

up above. So if we are going to accept that there may be some external, non-material source of goodness and love, it has to be a concept that makes sense and by which we can live.

But it's not just us, two women, saying it. A maverick Church of England vicar, the Rev Geraint ap Iorwerth, who presides over the church of St Peter ad Vincula, in Gwynedd, Wales, has also dedicated a church to the 'eternal feminine'.

An admirer, the journalist and broadcaster Ian Skidmore, wrote on his blog at Christmas, 2011:

People are still rewriting religious truths. A Welsh chum of mine, the Reverend Geraint ap Iorwerth, was never happy with a Holy Trinity of "two HEs and an It".

Forty years ago he founded the Order of Sancta Sophia which sees God as the Divine Feminine. Believers from all over the world visit first his website and then make pilgrimages to the Church of Wales' St Peter ad Vincula at Pennal, near Aberdovey, where he is rector. Ap Iorwerth told me: "People are fed up with traditional religious structures. The church is dying because most people live outside the old religious commitments. Less than eight per cent of people in Wales go to church or chapel on Sundays so there has got to be something wrong.

"I still function as a traditional Anglican priest for those who see me in that role, but I promote the ancient Celtic church as well. It was gentler and more tolerant. They are more in touch with the feminine and more akin to the Eastern Church. Praise and thanksgiving rather than doom, gloom and hell fire.

"The Wisdom of God, always feminine, can bring people together. She is almost like a Divine Consort. Pennal is where Christ and Sophia dance together."

The Rector says: "I don't think there is one true faith. The Cosmic Christ is beyond all religions. Who are we to limit his Person? He came to teach humility and we are arrogant to say there is no True Love in other religions.

"How can we claim an exclusive line to God when every religion gives you a different perspective of Truth? God would have been daft to leave it all to Christianity."

Geraint ap Iorwerth also found himself the subject of many news stories in July 2011, when he cut up certain passages from the St James Bible, in that year celebrating its tercentenary, and pasted them on an inside wall of his church, as a 'wall of shame' in protest at many of the sanctimonious references to its beautiful language.

Yes, he said, the language may be beautiful, but there is much cruelty and terror in the Bible and we have to think of the meaning behind the language. He cut up the bits of the Bible which highlighted a vengeful God and made them into a large collage.

Jayanti, who or what is God, do you think?

I see God as both the mother and the father, the eternal feminine and the eternal masculine, and have an understanding of God as a supreme being, a non-physical point of light that is neither male nor female, and certainly not patriarchal. The idea of a patriarchal God comes in with the notion of authority. In the traditional Christian view, God has authority over men and men have authority over women. It's the idea of God being male which has caused so many problems for women. But actually God is both the mother and the father in one person.

In the Old Testament, God is portrayed as being almost like a human, speaking directly to prophets, ordering them around, delivering the Ten Commandments and so on. Yet if you stop thinking of God as a person and view him instead as the ocean of love and happiness, forgiveness and compassion and the source of everything that's good, then to my mind at least, the notion of a God becomes much more acceptable.

Where do you stand on evolution and creationist theories?

I'll take the Creationist concept first, as it's easier to dismiss. I believe that nobody created either God or human beings, or other species come to that. If you start to believe in circular time, you can begin to appreciate that everything is eternal and is not created or destroyed. Yes, everything lives and dies and has its season, but in nature everything is eternally renewed. Scientists can accept this as well as religious people, because it is self-evident.

Evolution is a vastly more complex notion and has the weight of mainstream science behind it. It seems to me that although dinosaurs and other abnormal creatures certainly existed for a time, no great numbers of their bones have been found. And where is the evidence for the transitional species we hear about?

I think that evolution is an attractive idea for the ego as it gives the possibility that things are progressing and improving all the time. Don't forget either that theories of evolution first arose in the nineteenth century, when imperialism was at its height. It was fine for the ruling powers to rule because they were more 'evolved' than savages or subject races and therefore superior.

Evolution theories started when the earth was being exploited and there was no awareness of the earth as a living system. There was widespread exploitation and aggression, and the breakdown of the ecosystem started at about this time. Also, a few people controlled finances and exploited the rest of the world. Whatever you think about God, you can't argue with this.

As an Indian woman, I was made aware of how completely the British ignored the rich culture of our country, and dismissed all the teachings, scriptures, writings and traditions. All we were good for, it seemed, were our fantastic textiles, the Paisley patterns, intricate carpets and so on. Because they dismissed our intricate, complex culture, and considered Indians as lesser than themselves, the British considered it right and proper that they should rule the Indian races and pronounce Queen Victoria Empress of India.

This is what we used to sing about in Bishop Heber's hymn:

What tho' the spicy breezes
Blow soft o'er Ceylon's Isle
And every prospect pleases
And only man is vile.
In vain with lavish kindness
The gifts of God are strewn
The heathen in his blindness
Bows down to wood and stone.

And there is a statue to him in Calcutta! Mahatma Gandhi said in response, addressing some missionaries:

"You, the missionaries come to India thinking that you come to a land of heathens, of idolators, of men who do not know God. One of the greatest of Christian divines, Bishop Heber, wrote the two lines which have always left a sting with me: 'Where every prospect pleases, and man alone is vile.' I wish he had not written them. My own experience in my travels throughout India has been to the contrary. I have gone from one end of the country to the other, without any prejudice, in a relentless search after truth, and I am not able to say that here in this fair land, watered by the great Ganges, the Brahmaputra and the Jumna, man is vile. He is not vile. He is as much a seeker after truth as you and I are, possibly more so"

(from a speech at a Meeting of Missionaries at the Y.M C.A. Calcutta, Vol. 27 p. 434-39, Young India, 6-8-1925, October 8, 1925.)

Well, that was then, and evolution or not, Christians or not, it was totally a man's world in those days. But now that women are equal seekers after truth, where do you think God fits in?

As I see it, it is not as Creator, Avenger or Judge, but as the supreme source of everything that is good. God did not create the world of matter but remains outside it. The world of matter is eternal and although it changes, it is always there, running by its own energy. This is where I side with the evolutionists, that there is no God in the world of matter. Where I take issue is that at some point, it all started from nothing. It is eternal and as such, has no beginning or end.

So is God a part of us? If we have souls, are they an aspect of God?

No, God is not part of us but remains outside. We are not shards of light breaking off from God. There is a general idea in Eastern religions and also Christianity that all of us combine to make up God, that God is both within and without. To me, this idea does not make sense because it would mean there is no individual existence of the human being. If God is within all of us, this means that whatever I'm doing, God is doing too and there is no difference between good and evil.

All societies, whether primitive or sophisticated, have concepts of good and evil, systems of justice and of holding people accountable for their actions. If God is in everything, where is the accountability of human beings?

What, then, is evil? It is not a word we like to use much, nowadays.

Evil comes from ignorance, when we do not know how to behave because we don't know, or have forgotten, that we have a source of truth, love and goodness that we can tap into at any time. When human beings become ignorant of their human identity and associate purely with matter and materialism, this leads to negativity coming in. There are no higher values. We have seen how, in both Renaissance and Victorian times, rich bankers felt that they had to give something back, to make amends for all the riches they had amassed, and as a result they became great patrons of the arts, great philanthropists, and in many cases, gave all their wealth away because they feared the wrath of God otherwise. All traces of this consciousness have vanished with capitalists today.

Instead, so many people dedicate all their time and energy devising ways to rip others off.

If I start to forget that I am a soul, and start to believe I am only composed of physical matter, there is a loss of consciousness and this leads to bad behavior. These patterns intensify over time until we become trapped by negativity. The pattern started several centuries ago and has grown and grown until now, it is reaching its full extent.

Negative forces have multiplied and God's role at this time is to give us an understanding of who we are and how we can deal with the negativity that is threatening to envelop us. God will give us the power to free ourselves from these forces.

Yes, an American Unitarian Minister, the Rev G. Jude Geiger, wrote in the Huffington Post blog that Hell definitely exists, but that it's in the here and now rather than something reserved for the wicked beyond bodily death. He said:

I do believe in Hell. I just believe that it's in our lived experience and crafted by human hands. The news story of a Walmart shopper who was desperate enough to pepper spray fellow shoppers is a clear illustration of one kind of Hell. Pain and misery, both physical and emotional, is suffered because of a perceived lack. Life isn't full enough without the plastic-wrapped widget. It's almost as if the latest item on sale has become the biblical Golden Calf, the idol we build when we think God is absent. "If only we can obtain it, all will be well."

Whether you believe in an afterlife or not though, religious values can still be of help. If Hell is caused with the belief that we are fundamentally lacking something, then Heaven is found when we recognize the abundance before us that we have been given regardless of our own merit.

That is a strong statement from a Christian minister. It was echoed in an article written by the British Chief Rabbi, Jonathan Sachs, when he was about to visit the Pope in a historic meeting, to discuss how spiritual values have been completely lost from everyday life. Can you now give us some prime examples of negative patterns of behavior?

One of the greatest is greed, which is particularly manifesting itself in the world today. Greed is a state in which people are always needy, never satisfied but always have to have more. This is the standard condition of today. Many very rich people have more than enough but they must always acquire more. There is simply not enough money in the world for them.

Another is anger, which again is constantly growing in the world today. Although of course people have always been angry, it is the short fuse which is becoming ever more common, and some of these manifestations are quite new. A few years ago you never heard of road rage, office rage, supermarket rage, but now they are everyday concepts.

And only God can help us to remove these aspects of bad behavior?

Yes, they have become so ingrained that only God can help us to remove them. God is energy, luminous and one form that can never change. Education and financial freedom have now given women the power to break through, to embrace this concept of God and start to make real changes in the world. So we must take advantage of it, seize the moment.

Is God physically anywhere?

No, God is beyond the physical dimension. He resides in what we call the subtle regions.

What attributes does God possess?

God has a mind, intellect and a personality but no physical attributes at all.

Is there any way of proving God's existence?

No, we cannot prove. There are many things that science remains unable to measure, such as feelings, emotions, memory. And at present there is no way of proving God's existence that would satisfy hardcore scientists.

At some point an instrument may be invented which measures the human soul or at least the vibrations emanating from it and from there we may be able to show how God works, but if so, it will have to go way beyond any instruments we have at present. But I don't rule it out. Years ago there were no mobile phones, television, washing machines, computer chips, aeroplanes. They would have seemed like so much impossible magic to medieval people, for instance, who would have denied that such things might be possible. It may well be that in time, science will be able to validate the dimension beyond the physical.

his dimension we are talking about is that of souls, light and God. There are two ideas of Heaven that we have. One is the Heaven up above and the other is the Garden of Eden, or Heaven on Earth. The Heaven up above is a specific location and it is certainly within the realms of possibility that quantum physics will eventually be able to explain the soul and the soul world.

At the moment, all I can say is that many former atheists have come to us at the Brahma Kumaris and experienced a dimension beyond the physical, something they never remotely expected to happen. It has been such a reality to them that they have started to believe. It is difficult to explain this to people who have never had this experience, much as people who have never been passionately in love may dismiss it as a poetic fancy not grounded in any kind of reality.

By becoming secular, we have thrown out an actual relationship with God and loss of awareness or appreciation of the spiritual has led to our present condition of greed, ego and anger.

Is God omnipresent, omnipotent and omniscient?

God is not omnipresent. He resides and remains in one location where he acts as transmitter of all good qualities. Earth is the stage where humans take on physical form and play their part. God is not part of this scenario, neither does he interfere. God has his specific task to perform and humans have their part to play, and these remain separate.

Nor is God omnipotent. Human beings have choices whereby we make decisions. We have free will and we can choose our destiny. We must make our own choices and bear the consequences of those. God will not prevent people from doing wrong. And he does not send hurricanes or tornadoes to punish people. In fact, God does not punish people at all. There is no dreadful day of Judgment. We bring all bad actions, even those considered natural disasters, upon ourselves. So-called 'acts of God' are not acts of God but acts of humans and we have interfered with the mechanism of nature so that everything is in a state of upheaval.

But yes I do believe that God is omniscient. I believe that God knows everything. He knows what is going on in the hearts and minds of humans, through vibrations we are transmitting.

There are many superstitions of God that have grown up over the centuries, and one is that he controls every aspect of our lives. This is not true, and is one major reason why so many people have stopped believing in a God. They ask: if there is a God, how can he allow so much evil to happen? So many of the concepts of

God we've grown up with are not the reality and don't answer important questions.

The way people have understood God in the past has allowed the world to decline steadily.

So what is God's role?

At this time in the eternal cycle, God's role is to play the role of father, mother, teacher, guide, to enable us to restore an understanding of who we are. By teaching us how to meditate, we will discover, or rediscover, our own original qualities and purify and empower ourselves to the point where we can replace bad actions and behavior with good ones instead. As a result, a new world order can begin from the present chaos. The human soul will change, nature will change, but God never changes.

In the past, things have run on their own energy but this energy is now wearing down and there is nowhere for significant material growth to come from.

Because God is a stable force, in fact the only stable force, he can enable humans and nature to be restored back to what they should be. But only if we start to connect with him. It won't just happen by itself or without effort on our part.

You say that greed, anger and every kind of evil has grown and grown in the world today. Yet if we read ancient and medieval texts, many of those authors are saying exactly the same thing and that the wickedness of humans will lead to God destroying everything. The seven deadly sins is a very ancient concept and the Bible spends a lot of time telling how the Israelites will be separated from their wickedness thanks to the direct intervention of God.

This is true, and of course greed, anger, lust and all the other vices are not new. What is new is that aggression, violence and greed are now all global. There is more poverty than ever before. There is loss of values worldwide, there is suffering worldwide, the breakdown of the ecosystem is worldwide. Family structures have broken down. Even the nuclear family structure has broken down, never mind the extended family set up of the past. The bad behavior of leaders of most countries has made people lose faith in all institutions and the wrongdoing of religious leaders has turned people away from God.

The financial breakdowns of recent years have been totally caused by going away from God and eliminating all values from the world of commerce. There is discontent everywhere and no spiritual awareness which might give inner contentment and due recognition of other human beings. The breakdown of the environment is, as I see it, also related to the spiritual crisis. In the paradigm of materialism, people simply do not see the inter-connectedness of everything.

And women are better at seeing this connectedness?

Yes, definitely. Or to put it another way, the feminine principle is better at interconnectedness. Once we acknowledge who and what God is, we can start to see the bigger picture. Whatever I do, for good or bad, sends out ripples that have consequences. Virtually nothing happens in isolation and so every little bit of negativity has a wide impact. Yet with God's input, love, truth, power and order can be restored to the world.

Now, God is calling on women to lead the way and although some men are not going to like this, it's how it is going to have to be. It is women's role now to usher in the new age. In the past, if women had tried to come to the fore, nobody would have listened and it's not until women arrived at this present stage of being educated and independent, that this change can happen. Women cannot now follow men or even walk beside them, but must overtake. It is only when women are able to make choices in life that they are able to make a difference.

Do you think that the militant atheists have in a sense prepared the way, opened us up to this new concept of God?

Yes, I do. The books by Dawkins, Hitchens and other atheists have received such widespread publicity and their authors have been on many radio and TV shows that they have made people start to think about these vital issues. The debate has opened up but until now, the vital role of women in helping people turn to God has not come to the fore.

Chapter Seven

More Awkward Questions Answered

The essence of what we have discussed so far can be summed up as:

1   Women now have to take charge, both of themselves and in the wider world;

2   For the first time in history, women are uniquely placed to be able to do this;

3   The feminine principle of harmony and interconnectness needs to replace the old, outdated masculine principle of divide and conquer, rule and subdue;

4   In order to bring about the required transformation, a change of consciousness is required;

5   This change requires us to admit spirituality back into our lives;

6   By spirituality, we mean having an awareness of the vibrations of love, goodness, compassion and justice;

7   Transformation of the right kind is achieved by regular meditation;

8   l allow us 'time out' of our busy lives and enable the true self to be realized;

9   Through meditation, we may well come to have an awareness that somebody or something out there is trying to make contact with us;

10   That somebody is God, the source of all wisdom and love;

11   Once the connection with God is established, then powerful changes for good can be made;

12   None of this is possible while leading a completely secular, materialistic life. Unless spirituality is recognized

and acknowledged, things can only get worse.

In the explanation we are offering in this book, God is separate and different from human beings, but all humans have a divine spark within them, usually known as the soul, which is the eternal aspect of themselves and which never dies. It is the soul that will connect with God through the practice of meditation.

One major reason for some Christians and religious fundamentalists being so against abortion is that they believe the soul enters the embryo at the moment of conception, and so by aborting a fetus, we are killing an eternal soul as well or at least, depriving it of the opportunity to come to term as a human being. For atheists, who do not believe in the soul, there should be no such problem.

According to Middle Eastern religions, the human soul has one physical birth, after which it ascends into heaven (or descends into hell perhaps) for all eternity. 'One short sleep past, we wake eternally' as John Donne put it.

Far Eastern religions by contrast believe that the soul will reincarnate into a succession of physical bodies, according to its karma, or the ancient law of cause and effect that determines successive incarnations.

In Buddhism, souls can work their way out of all wickedness by living according to the Noble Eightfold Path, and eventually attain a state known as Nirvana, when they are pure soul and never have to take another body.

We are not here to convert the unbelievers, who can no doubt blind us with science, but we hope that this chapter will shed some further light on questions and dilemmas that have exercised thinkers and seekers throughout the ages, and which have never satisfactorily been explained away by said scientists.

What exactly is the soul?

As we see it, the soul is composed of three non-physical

elements, the mind, intellect and tendencies. The tendencies, known as *sanskaras* in Sanskrit, refer to the imprints received in previous incarnations and which will determine the next incarnation.

As the soul is not a physical entity, it cannot be created or destroyed but unlike God, who is unchanging, the soul changes according to its various incarnations. It is understood in Eastern religions to be located at the point between the eyes, although this is not a physical location. It is the soul which will determine the role we will enact in any incarnation although of course, environmental, hereditary and cultural factors also play their part.

Can it ever make sense to militant atheists and evolutionary biologists?

Probably not. Our belief is that the soul takes precedence over physical forms but if you don't accept that there is a soul then there is nowhere to go. For such people, death is the end and a human being is just a human being. There is no comeback, there are no far reaching consequences, therefore there is no incentive to behave well, and no impetus to make life on earth better. If everything comes about by pure chance and there is no rhyme or reason in anything, then it doesn't really matter how badly you behave. You may be caught by the law of the land if you steal or kill, but you might not. You may get away with it. Many do.

If however, you believe that there always is a comeback for your actions according to the law of karma, then there is a great incentive to behave well.

Can you describe and explain karma? Obviously it is a very complicated doctrine, but just in simple terms, for those who may be new to the idea?

In Sanskrit the word karma means 'action' and we understand it to be the inexorable law of cause and effect. Karma is something we humans create for ourselves and does not involve God. In Christianity, the idea of karma is encapsulated in the expression, as you sow, so shall you reap.

This means that whatever we do, will come back to us in some form. Eastern religions understand three kinds of karma: good karma, bad karma and neutral karma. Some actions are so neutral that their consequences will usually be minimal, such as washing and dressing in the morning, shopping, saying hello to a neighbor. The more complex the action, the more likely there will be a karmic comeback.

Good karma results from good actions such as kindness, compassion, love, benevolence and trust, whereas bad karma results from the vices we have mentioned, such as greed, anger, lust and dishonesty. Whatever you do in life, something will come back to you from that action. Again, there is a useful phrase in Christianity to explain this: cast thy bread upon the waters and it will come back to you after many years.

Sometimes we set a train of events in action where the comeback is not noticed for many years or decades. But we should never imagine we have got away with anything. It may be that the results of certain actions will only become apparent in future incarnations.

There is the idea, in many religions, that God has placed us in our stations, class or caste and that we must be content with this. But what we have to take on board is that at the moment of birth there are currently such discrepancies, such vast differences in health, wealth, opportunities in life that the question arises: is all this merely a matter of chance?

Is it God who creates all this unfairness? Is it the parents? Is it the genes? Heredity? Environment? You may ask of a child who is born in miserable or abusive surroundings: what have they done to deserve it? Equally, you may wonder what a child has done to deserve being brought up happy and healthy, with loving parents and given every advantage. Is it purely the luck of the draw?

If you are prepared to take on board the idea of karma, then these discrepancies begin to make more sense. A person may, throughout their life, have done a lot of evil or caused a great deal of suffering which has not been accounted for in his or her life. Yes, heredity, genes and environment all play their part but there must be other forces at work that explain the great discrepancies we find today.

According to the law of karma, you create the conditions in one life that determine your situation in the next. Karma is not, as many people imagine, a system of reward and punishment. God does not punish a wicked person by making him blind or handicapped in the next incarnation. We create these conditions for ourselves. It is this notion that God punishes people for bad actions which has turned many people away from God. But if my actions are being returned in like kind, whether good or bad, this doesn't need God to be involved.

In traditional Eastern thought, it is considered a kind of punishment to be incarnated as a woman. Indian scriptures say that while there is rejoicing at the birth of a baby boy, a baby girl is not welcomed as she is only a liability. Much of this idea remains, even among professed atheists. The idea that a female is a lesser being than a male still lingers on in most cultures, even the most secular.

To me, the fact that there are so many imponderables in human existence indicate something beyond, both before and after bodily birth and death. The doctrines of karma and reincarnation go together and are inextricably bound up. You work through your karma through your successive births and there is the opportunity, in each birth, to improve your karma for your next birth.

Is there any strong evidence of reincarnation or karma at work? Or is it just something we have to believe?

At the moment it's only anecdotal but it is also observational. There is the well-described phenomenon of déjà vu, where you have the strong feeling you have been to this place before, even though you know you haven't. Of course, people will dismiss this by saying you must have seen it on a film, or read about it in a book and it has made such a strong impression you think you've been there before. It has never been possible to explain away every incidence of déjà vu like this, though. There are instances of people being able to describe a place intimately, including all the layout and buildings, and they get goose pimples as they approach it.

There is also the phenomenon of meeting somebody for the very first time with whom you have an instant strong connection. Although you have never met them before you instantly seem to know everything about them and you are immediately very close to each other. The other person also feels this connection. Again, it has never been fully explained by biologists or other scientists. Yes, it could be something like brain waves merging, and there could be a physical explanation, but nobody has ever yet come up with one. For those who believe in previous lives and karma, such a meeting indicates that there is unfinished business between you, business that you now have to complete.

There are also the experiments carried out by the late American psychology professor Ian Stevenson, where he investigated claims by children who seemed to have remembered previous lives. This research is hard to ignore, and was very thorough. Professor Stevenson chose to research claims by children, as they would have little to gain by apparently remembering past lives. In some cases, adults have made these claims a part of showbiz and this is one of the problems about taking them seriously.

There are also a number of books where people have been taken back into past lives by hypnotherapists, and described what happened to them in a past age. Additionally, there is also the phenomenon of people being put under hypnosis and being able to speak in languages they don't know in their everyday lives.

Yes, there was a famous book about a group of present day people having been Cathars, in the middle ages, and being able to speak in the langue d'oc, a kind of medieval French. There are also the bestselling books by Brian Weiss, an American psychiatrist, who has taken people back into past lives.

Then there are the novels of Joan Grant, popular in their day, which relied on her 'far memory' to describe life in ancient Egypt, Renaissance Italy and so on. Although originally sold as fiction, Joan later said they were her own past life experiences, and that she had actually been the heroines of her books. There is quite a lot of literature to support the idea of reincarnation, but it is dismissed by scientists and atheists as complete and utter rubbish, believed in only by the gullible.

I witnessed one person being put under hypnosis, where she revealed she was the incarnation of Ruth Ellis, the last woman to be hanged in Britain. Under hypnosis, she spoke of her obsessive love for David Blakely, the man she killed.

Now, whether there is anything in all these stories I can't say, but I would imagine it would be difficult to dismiss every single one, and most of the detractors have never read a single one of these books or listened to the stories. But it's easy to put them into the realms of fantasy and science fiction.

That's true. It's not easy to prove the reality of what these people are saying or alleging. But what we do know is that from the moment of birth, the child brings its own characteristics and personality, not all of which can be explained in terms of genetics, and it certainly can't be explained in terms of environment because so far, there is no environment. Yet however many children you have, they will all be completely different from each other, even though they share a gene pool and environment.

It seems to me that children bring much with them and that they do not start off life as a blank slate on which everything is subsequently written. If this was the case, there would be much less variety in human beings than we actually have.

But stories and recollections apart, the fact is that if we accept the law of karma, we open the way towards creating a world of justice. Karma offers an explanation for all the injustice in the world, and gives tools to start to change this. It means that we have a sense of responsibility for our actions, on the basis that whatever we do, will cause a ripple of action and reaction.

Some Eastern religions believe that we can be incarnated into other life forms such as those of animals or even insects. Do you believe this to be true?

No. Our belief is that humans will always take another human life form. In the East it is often believed that the soul progresses through different species, and this ancient belief has a tie-up with the much later theory of evolution, excluding the soul aspect of this progression. But it seems much more logical that the human soul always needs a human, as it is so intricate and so much more intricate than the souls of even the highest animals, assuming they have a soul.

Too many unanswerable questions arise if you believe the soul progresses through different species, such as: If I am an animal, say a sheepdog or guide dog for the blind, and as such I do lots of good karma, do I then become a human? But what good karma can a dog or a donkey perform to ensure a higher birth next time? A dog does not choose to be put in the service of humans; that is something their owners and trainers decide for them.

Alternatively, if I do bad things as a human, is my punishment to be reincarnated as an animal? I don't feel deprived if I'm a donkey, as I just then live the life of a beast of burden. It's probably best not to get into the areas of pure speculation as to whether other species work their way through karma of their own. How can we ever know?

One problem with this idea of souls taking on successive human births is that there are many more people around than, say, five hundred years ago. Where do all these new souls come from?

Our belief in the Brahma Kumaris is that new souls are coming into incarnation all the time. There is the concept of 'new souls' and 'old souls' that people speak about, even if they don't actually believe in the soul. According to this concept, an 'old soul' will be a much more multi-layered person than a new soul, which does not yet contain all the imprints of previous births. A new soul, as we see it, will be somebody for whom everything goes right and they will have an easy passage through life. They will not have to endure struggles and reversals of fortune, by contrast with old souls that have accumulated a lot of past karma. This is one explanation of how people are so very different from each other.

Now here is a very difficult question: will new souls keep coming down forever? If so, there will hardly be standing room on the planet. Or will we move to live on other planets by then? There is no indication that the world population is decreasing, in spite of initiatives by many countries to limit population growth.

Most religions have an idea of eventual destruction, or Armageddon, and the phrase, 'the end of the world is nigh' although often spoken jokingly, is known to all. People don't like to believe this will happen, but ever more people feel that nowadays, we are sitting on a time bomb, and that there will be some kind of all-out nuclear war. When you have suicide bombers who have no regard for their own lives or anybody else's, anything is possible.

We believe that eventually there will be some sort of destruction, or Holocaust, which will destroy practically everything and that this will be a nuclear war of some kind. The weapons of mass destruction already in existence will eventually be put to use.

But not everybody will perish by any means, and by the time this happens, the new world order we have been talking about, will be ready to come into being.

With women at the head?

Jayanti (laughing) Of course! In our version of the Garden of Eden, men and women will be completely equal. There will be no idea of woman coming out of the rib of a man.

I appreciate that this is a difficult concept for many people to accept and it is easy to laugh at it and dismiss it as so much superstitious nonsense. But even the most hardline atheists and evolutionary biologists must accept that world population simply cannot go on growing at its present rate, and that there will not possibly be enough resources for everybody. Plus we cannot ignore climate change, nor can anybody tell us how we are going to climb back to financial stability. It certainly won't happen while we carry on as we are doing.

Is there any proof or evidence of what you are saying?

No, we cannot prove any of it. Some people believe that nature always rights itself, somehow, and that might happen of course. Nobody knows for sure. But we don't believe that the apocalypse will be caused by God intervening in human affairs. We believe that humans will bring about their own destruction.

A book called *The Limits to Growth*, written in 1972 by three American computer scientists, warned that we had to curb

growth or risk complete meltdown of the planet by the year 2000. This was not a religious or spiritual book, but used a computer model by which it compared and contrasted linear with exponential growth and concluded that there would eventually be overshoot and collapse and a complete collapse of global civilization. The two elements, the authors thought, that would bring about collapse were population growth and climate change. Of course the book was laughed out of court at the time and the world did not end by the year 2000, but it seems, from what you are saying, that we are rapidly approaching a time when these predictions, based solely on a computer model are actually coming true.

Well, there you are. Common sense tells us that resources are finite, that the planet cannot support an infinite number of people, and 'there must eventually be overshoot and collapse.

Do you believe that Jesus was the Son of God?

Jesus was a very great prophet, as were Abraham and Mohammed. They are all sons of God, and dispensed much wisdom. They possibly had a more direct line to God than ordinary humans but they were all a hundred per cent human and born in the usual way.

Where do you stand on spiritualism, or attempts to contact the dead? Does it have any connection with spirituality?

Spiritualism has nothing to do with spirituality, which is to do with understanding the self and the divine. Spiritualism, which purports to contact dead people, is just playing around and serves no purpose. But yes, I do believe that communication with the dead is possible. If you believe that the soul is eternal then theoretically it may be possible to make contact with the recently dead. But it creates a disturbance to the spirit being contacted. Again, atheists will say there is no such thing and there is no explanation that will satisfy them.

It only seems possible to contact the dead if there has been a deep bond between you; if the dead person is a relative or spouse for instance. In situations where there has been a sudden death, untimely death, a murder, for example, the living often have a strong desire to connect with that person. This is frequently done through a medium and I definitely believe the recently dead can be contacted, but that there is no point in doing so. It does not achieve anything.

There have been many recorded instances where a recently dead person has come and visited the living. It happened to a friend of mine. Her husband died suddenly and unexpectedly and she was consumed with grief. She told me that he had come back three times to visit her and sat in his favorite chair. She was not a spiritual person or a believer. Would something like this be so much delusion? Nobody else could see him.

When somebody comes back like this, it's where there has been deep attachment and a deep bond. The relationship has not fully concluded itself at the moment of death and yes, the soul, the ethereal body, is actually in that room. Again, although there is a lot of anecdotal evidence of this happening, there is no explanation that would satisfy an atheist.

What about psychics, people who believe they can see spirits?

Some people can definitely see auras and this indicates some kind of energy level and they can sometimes also contact the recently dead. The person they contact is almost always a close relative of the living. But what I ask is: does this make those still living better people, more spiritual individuals? There are also those who can read people's minds, hear what they are thinking and feel what they are feeling. Again, this is an actual ability that some people have and it's not just a tiny minority. But as BKs, we believe it is dangerous to try to read other people's minds and get right inside their thought processes. It's as if bits of them are brushing off on you, and you have to take steps to shut it down. **Then there is the near-death experience, which is well documented.**

Yes, there has now been much research and many books written on the subject. The near-death experience describes a state where the soul is separate from the body, where it leaves the body but because the body is not quite ready for death, the soul returns back into it. Those who have had such an experience describe a world of light, a warm and welcoming place where they have a recognition of God.

Modern medicine has made the near-death experience not just a reality, but relatively common and all the evidence is hard to dismiss.

For everybody who has had such an experience, their lives are completely changed. They become less selfish more spiritual, more caring and less afraid of death.

De Peter Fenwick is a neuropsychiatrist who had so much evidence of the near-death experience from his patients he decided to investigate it for himself, using scientific methods. He was a hardcore scientist, a non-believer, and his research completely changed his beliefs.

The International Association for Near-Death Studies holds regular conferences on science and spirituality and is the nearest we have yet to a scientific approach to the possibility of the existence of the soul.

A note on the Near-Death Experience
The term was first coined in 1975 by American psychiatrist Dr Raymond Moody, to describe an out-of-the-body experience several of his patients had undergone when near death. They described entering a world of light and an encounter with an unconditionally loving light and a sense of watching themselves with a consciousness that was not connected with their bodies. Sometimes, thanks to modern resuscitation techniques, these people were brought back from near-death and

continued to live in their bodies for a long time afterwards. In every instance, they were profoundly altered by the experience.

Dr Moody decided to set up an organization to research and report on the Near-Death Experience in a scientific manner, and IANDS was set up in America in the late 1970s. It unleashed a stream of publicity all round the world, and many people came forward to tell their stories.

IANDs has been in existence for over three decades now and people often ask whether the NDE is proof of life after death. Their official response is that as the NDE is subjective, it cannot be measured, observed and tested by somebody else. The organization says that the experience does suggest that there is some aspect of human consciousness that it unconnected with the body but that at present, no means currently exists to demonstrate whether or not this speculation is true.

To date, several million people all over the world have described NDEs; the first recounted by Plato in The Republic, written around 420 BC.

Those who experience an NDE are not necessarily religious; they come from all backgrounds, cultures and societies, but their descriptions of the NDE are remarkably similar. In a small number of cases, the experience is negative and is found to be harrowing and negative To date, there has been no scientific or evolutionary explanation of the NDE'

On the other hand, academic Dr Susan Blackmore, who herself had a dramatic out of the body experience as a young woman and as a result spent the next 30 years researching psychic phenomena, has concluded that there are no psychic phenomena, but only wishful thinking, deception, experimental error and occasionally, fraud. "None of it ever gets anywhere," she wrote of her researches. Susan is now an atheist, member of the British Humanist Society and derides religion for its idea of a creator God, virgin births, the subservience of women, transubstantiation and all the other trappings which are 'backed up by untestable but ferocious rewards and punishments.'

Well, that is precisely the old-fashioned and largely unacceptable *idea of God and religion that we have been trying to knock down in this book, and replace with something far more female-friendly and workable for present-day society.*

Why are so many people concerned to assert that there is no God?

Atheists primarily believe they are saving the world from illusion, from superstition, myth and fairy tale and substituting it with reality. They are committed to their beliefs and genuinely believe they are doing the world a service. And in many ways they have because they have encouraged people to read their books and think harder about religion than they might have done otherwise.

But in conclusion, if we genuinely want the world to be a better place, we must accept the reality of the individual human soul and the reality of God?

Yes, at this moment in time there is no other way forward.

Conclusion

Although we may not have all the answers, we hope that we have provided a new, workable perspective on the eternal questions which people have asked since – well, since people began asking questions, and have, at least to some extent, filled the 'God-shaped hole' that many now feel inside them.

We also hope to have made a convincing case as to why it has to be up to women to show the way forward, and that in order to combat the rapidly rising levels of greed, lust, ego and violence in the world, we must embrace some kind of spirituality.

But we cannot turn back the clock. Traditional, old-style patriarchal religions are exhausted and need to be replaced by a modern, logical, no-fuss form of spirituality. And as women are more naturally inclined than men to spirituality, it stands to reason that women must now be at the forefront. Plus, women have much less attachment than men to the old ways, as these never benefitted women much anyway.

The female-centered spirituality we have been describing, which puts the feminine values of compassion, humility, gentleness and love, centre stage, is, as we see it, the only option now left to us.

The secularization that advanced apace in the twentieth century was necessary to enable women, for the first time in history, to become educated, independent and poised to make a mark in the wider world. Contraception freed us from the burden of endless childbearing, abortion meant we did not have to bring an unwanted child into the world, and divorce meant that we were no longer tied for life in a dreadful marriage.

These were all major advances for women, and enabled us to take a more significant place in the world.

And as I write, there are already hopeful signs that we may be on the way to a more female-friendly society.

In some countries women are now already making major waves. In Norway, for instance, since 2002, women have had to make up at least 40 per cent of all board members on companies quoted on the Norwegian stock exchange. This quota was ushered in as a result of positive discrimination laws and is now being implemented by other countries, such as Holland, Germany, Spain and France.

Why? Because, belatedly, men are realizing that it makes a difference – in a good way - to have a significant number of women in the boardroom. Women think and behave differently from men and in boardrooms, this is a distinct advantage. Women ask more questions and do not regard themselves so much as know alls. At the same time, men are more prepared to stick their necks out and take risks, so the input of both types of behavior is important.

As a result of Norway's stand on having more women in the boardroom, the small Nordic country is one of the most economically successful in the world, with productivity higher than any other country. Many commentators believe this is directly attributable to the large numbers of women in influential positions on company boardrooms, and point out that many, if not most, of the disgraced companies over the past few years, such as Eon, Lehman Brothers, Enron, for example, had an all-male or virtually all-male board at the time of their collapse. Any woman on the board was just a token presence.

Just about all the disgraced bankers who pocketed huge salaries and bonuses while taking wild risks with customers' deposits, were also men.

On another point, Norwegian women are seen as the most beautiful and desirable on international dating sites. Why? Because of their confidence and self-esteem! Women there have been given a chance, and they have responded by pulling their full weight to advance the economic prosperity of the country. Some studies also suggest that Norwegian women are the happiest in the world, as well. Norway also has a high number of women at senior levels in government, police, civil service and education.

This example just shows what can happen when women are given an equal opportunity; everything improves, even for men. And yet Norwegian men sitting on company boards admit that the quota would not have happened by itself, as they would never voluntarily have conceded power.

In another example, most of the senior management team at the British department store Selfridges, one of the leading stores in the world, is female, black or gay. As a result, this store has become one of the most innovative and successful retail companies of all time. By contrast, most of the retail stores and chains that have failed in recent years have been top-heavy with men.

Yet none of this would have happened, in Norway, Selfridges or anywhere else, if traditional religions had retained their power and women continued to be regarded as inferior. As we have seen, countries which still see women as second-class and homosexuals as hardly human, thanks to their religion, are among the most backward and repressive in the world, with around 90 per cent of the population at or below the poverty line while the rulers live in sumptuous palaces.

President Pratibha Patil, of India, the first woman ever to hold this office, said in her address in New Delhi in January 2012:

I strongly believe that women need to be drawn fully into the national mainstream. Empowerment of women will have a very big impact on creating social structures that are stable. The National Mission on Empowerment of Women set up in 2010, should help in the co-coordinated delivery of women-centric and women-related programmes. An important component of women's development is their economic and social security. Social prejudices prevalent in our society which have led to gender discrimination need to be corrected. Social evils like female foeticide, child marriage and dowry must be eradicated. Status of women is an important indicator of progress in a society.

All this is excellent stuff and shows that, all over the world it is being recognized that modern societies can only progress when women are empowered and encouraged.

Personal note: when I first visited India in 1984, it seemed unthinkable that a woman could ever be President. Granted, Indira Gandhi was then the Prime Minister, but she was the daughter of Pandit Nehru, India's first prime minister, and therefore in the line of dynasty. Her son Rajiv succeeded her. Pratibha Patil was an 'outsider' who worked her way up through the ranks by sheer merit.

But also as we have seen, although education and empowerment are important, they can only go so far.

The recent spate of anti-God books have drawn welcome attention to the deficiencies of traditional religions and beliefs about God, yet none of them give any useful guidelines about how to live our lives. They are more concerned with shooting down antiquated belief systems and misplaced faith, than helping us to build up a new, improved society from the ashes of the old. Richard Dawkins seems to think that appreciation of the beauty and intricacy of nature will lead us to live better lives, and that we do not need some supernatural creator to teach us about morals, ethics and good behavior.

So far, there is no sign whatever of that happening.

Nor can atheist tomes or scientific research give us any moral or ethical guidelines as to how to proceed in the future. But now, we have a framework whereby we can have these guidelines, and that is by connecting personally to God through meditation and contemplation.

Some people believe that ethical and moral standards can

apply without recourse to God, that we can just take the good aspects of religion without buying into any of the fairy-tale, mythical or supernatural elements. Books like Brian Mountford's *Christian Atheist* and Alain de Botton's *Religion for Atheists*, make out a good case for living ethically without the need for a religious or scriptural framework, but Jayanti maintains that without acknowledging God, we will inevitably slip back into a world where there is no accountability and no compassion. Even when women come to the fore, and the feminine qualities prevail, daily practice, daily discipline and connection is still needed to bring about lasting change in much the same way that one needs to go to the gym every day to maintain physical fitness. Maintenance of spiritual fitness requires similar daily dedication.

And over the past few decades, women have banked up a lot of anger against men and the patriarchal systems they erected. This anger needs to dissipate to allow positive qualities to come through.

By taking on board this modern concept of spirituality, we will be able to move forward without the anger and hatred against men that characterized many feminist tomes and tracts of the 1970s. Mind, they were necessary too, at the time. Centuries of oppression and subjection made twentieth-century woman very angry indeed but now we have the tools to take our rightful places without anger and resentment.

According to Jayanti, the first thing that will happen through regular meditation is that you will learn to love yourself, and from that everything else follows. The next thing is that you will start to experience love from other people. It is love that sets people free from the negative qualities of animosity, jealousy, greed, ego and attachment, and enables them to let go of the past. Love was very much at the heart of early Christianity, and it now needs to regain its central place in our lives.

And God, as we now understand him, is the alchemist who

brings about the transformation.

But we haven't finished yet. It is not easy to achieve and maintain heightened awareness while we cling on to old ways of thinking and relating to people. The first thing that must happen is to let go of attachment, the state of being intimately bound up with other people's states of mind, so that if they are angry, we are angry, if they are jealous, we feel jealous.

Women are particularly prone to attachment, to want to form a close, committed relationship with another person, and to merge with them so that boundaries become blurred. This is a condition that has come to be known as codependency, where you may actually think you *are* the other person, and for centuries this has been encouraged in women, with the idea that they subsume themselves into another identity on marriage, symbolized by a change of surname and the prefix 'Mrs'.

No such changes have ever been expected of men. They have been allowed to retain every scrap of their previous identity and it is only in recent years, in the West at least, that they too have worn wedding rings. But the days of women being the secondary or passive partner in marriage, are over, or are in their death throes at least. In India, the secondary status of wives was underlined by a woman accompanying her husband on an official engagement, to be known as 'wife of' or W/O.

Even if it was the woman who was the official, her husband was never referred to as 'husband of' or H/O but was always given the dignity of his own identity. In countries where women have equal education and equal access to jobs, they are far less likely to want to take their status from their husband's job or position. As the American feminist Gloria Steinem said some years ago, 'we can become the men we wanted to marry', meaning that we can have our own status rather than bathing in reflected glory.

True, in countries such as Norway, women are still in relationships, but these are no longer seen as the entire focus of their existence.

Along with spirituality and the empowerment that is received by connection with God, must go significant lifestyle and attitudinal changes.

It is also important, when on the path of self-transformation, to pay close attention to diet, on the understanding, supported by much research, that what feeds the body, will also feed the mind.

We now know that the type of food we eat intimately affects thought processes, emotions and also physical health. The ways that a really bad diet can adversely affect all physical and mental systems was dramatically shown up in the 2004 film, *Super Size Me*, where the documentary film maker Morgan Spurlock ate nothing but Big Macs, all the while tracking the changes that happened to him.

He not only gained weight but experienced mood swings and psychological problems as the diet continued. Spurlock, who made the film to demonstrate the means by which big corporations are persuading the world to eat an unhealthy diet for pure profit, was able to lose weight and overcome his mental health problems only by sticking to a gourmet vegan diet for 14 months after completing the Big Mac experiment on himself.

The problems of obesity and unhealthy eating are endemic in our society, particularly in poor countries. In Papua New Guinea, for instance, around 90 per cent of the population is obese. It is the same story with Maoris in New Zealand and aborigines in Australia. And once again, it is mainly women who suffer from the problems related to obesity.

This is not a book about diet, but according to the Brahma Kumaris, diet plays an integral part in achieving the kind of enhanced awareness we have been talking about in this book. The type of diet that will most change thinking is vegetarian, avoiding all meat and fish products.

Women seem to find it easier than men to stick to a vegetarian diet and as women are still mainly responsible for the food put on a family's table, they can easily take the lead here. Meat eating is associated with aggression but these days, meat often comes to us as the result of cruelty. Nor is it as healthy as in the past. The charity Compassion in World Farming has stated that the standard supermarket chicken consists of 70% fat, entirely caused by the dreadful diets fed to battery hens.

At one time it was quite difficult to eat a vegetarian diet but these days it is easy and most restaurants now offer vegetarian options. The BKs go further and say that we should not eat eggs, onions or garlic or any foods from the onion family.

The ban on onions is a tenet of some traditional branches of Hinduism and no dishes containing these are served in any BK centers. The reason for the ban is an ancient belief that these strong-tasting foods can incite lust and even possibly violence.

Of course alcohol is also forbidden in strict Hinduism and Islam. Very many fundamentalist Christian movements such as the Mormons, Seventh-Day Adventists, 'bible belt' Christians in America and Jehovah's Witnesses also ban alcohol

For many of us, wine is an enhancement to meals and social occasions, and we can take it in moderation. But again, worldwide, alcoholism is becoming a very serious problem. It is widespread among Australian aborigines and indigenous Americans and also a growing problem among young people and students.

Gambling is another vice we should not indulge in, including buying lottery tickets. Again, many religions hold that getting money without effort is wrong and forbid gambling. Increasingly, people have forgotten that gambling was once held to be a sin and now consider it part of everyday life. The governments of most countries have state lotteries, with huge wins possible, if unlikely. The growth of casinos and super-casinos has added to the problem, and online gambling is now very big business.

We should also not be part of the sex industry or pornography, even passively, by watching porn on the internet. Pornography is based on the notion that other people, and their sexuality, are marketable commodities. Once this idea takes hold, it opens the door to endless exploitation, cruelty and abuse. Prostitutes working in the legal brothels in Nevada, America, are mainly very young, displaced or mentally handicapped women. They may not be technically trafficked, but it is almost impossible for them to escape. Sadism can easily creep in where large sums of money change hands.

Nowadays, there are many websites offering 'escorts' for the evening or for the night. Although most of these escorts are women, men are on offer too, charging large sums for their services. None of this has anything to do with spirituality, elevating your life or thought processes and provides yet one more instance of the degradation into which we have sunk.

And it probably goes without saying that illegal recreational drugs should be given a wide berth.

All this may sound rather like the stern behavioral strictures ordained by God in the Old Testament, except that in those days, fast food outlets, fizzy drinks and highly processed snacks had not been invented, although they did have prostitutes and most likely, gambling, in Biblical times. There are many palaces, now mostly ruined, in Jordan, where rich men took prostitutes and courtesans to indulge in all kinds of decadent behavior, so we know this is nothing new. But now, it is universal and available to all with the click of a mouse.

The reason is that none of these things actually enhance life and eventually, only serve to make us more miserable. They are all addictions and if we are not careful, may eventually control us.

In its 75-year history, the BKs have had many former and current alcoholics, drug addicts, gamblers, criminals, murderers and all kinds of sinners and addicts coming to their centers.

Many have completely turned their lives around by the practice of meditation.

The reason for banning these practices is not to be a killjoy but rather, to enable people to have a clear, unclouded mind in order to gain higher perceptions.

One very contentious area the Brahma Kumaris addresses is that of sex and celibacy. Although there has been a long tradition of celibacy in the Christian church, with nuns and monks vowing to live a life of celibacy, there has been none in Hinduism, for women at least.

Hinduism has never had any tradition of the religious or spiritual life for women, although it is there for men, who are allowed to forsake their families and pursue a holy life after family responsibilities are over, or even to become ascetics with no possessions, begging for their food. So it was a total shock to tradition when the early BK women embraced celibacy, saying that they were now married to God and not to an earthly husband. Such a thing had never been known or even thought of in India before.

Now, it is accepted in India that surrendered BKs, both men and women, will be single and unmarried or, if married, will live together without sex. In the early days, many who eventually surrendered were married, in arranged marriages, but nowadays, most will choose to remain single and dedicate their lives to God.

Strictly speaking, all those seeking a strong connection with God, should be celibate, they say, in much the same way as Christian priests, monks and nuns dedicating their lives to God should also be celibate. We now know that in Christianity at least, that rule is often broken but it seems easier for women than men to abstain from sexual activity. Tantric sex has been regarded in some quarters as 'spiritual', leading to greater awareness, and it was practiced in the ashrams of Bhagwan Shree Rajneesh, an Indian mystic who attracted large numbers of Western adherents in the 1970s and 80s, possibly for this reason.

But the movement collapsed in murders, suicides, tax evasion, imprisonment, embezzlement and fraud.

The point about all the recommended lifestyle adjustments, Jayanti maintains, is that the struggle to bring about self-transformation and ultimately, world transformation, requires a new way of thinking and behaving, and this requires drastic alterations to existing patterns of thought and behavior, many of which are considered quite normal in the world today.

Clearly not everybody is going to be able to follow these guidelines to the letter and not everybody is going to be willing or able to follow the austere lifestyle recommended. It is a counsel of perfection, but Jayanti believes that once the practice of meditation and connection is established, the desire for these addictive externals will gradually fade away. It all starts, she says, from thinking of yourself as a soul, rather than as a body, as the driver rather than the car.

Once you can do this, you will take care of your body and not seek ways to abuse it.

This is the mental shift that must happen to make transformation possible, to regard yourself as a soul housed in a body rather than a body which may (or may not) have a soul. Once this is achieved, all thoughts of superiority and inferiority fade away. A child is a soul in a small body; an Indian or African is a soul in a brown or black body; a woman becomes a soul in a female body. Armed with this perception, all gender, class and body stereotypes will disappear and we will no longer judge people by their external appearance. Nor will some people be regarded as second class, or lower down the food chain, than others.

Again, this was a tenet of early Christianity, but the idea we are all equal before God was certainly not practiced, or not for very long. Hierarchies were soon established and although Christ may have considered women equal to men, the church established in his name did not.

Yes of course there remain vast differences between human

beings and we are not all equal in intelligence, beauty, talent, education and attainments. But if we come to regard everybody as our brother, or sister, then we can start to look beyond these differences.

The BKs have a popular saying: when I change, the world changes. Of course, it all takes a mighty and prolonged effort but with God's help it can be done.

The Brahma Kumaris

The Brahma Kumaris World Spiritual University is the only major spiritual movement in the world to be headed by women. It began life in Hyderabad, Sind, in the 1930s when a retired millionaire jeweler known as Dada Lekhraj began experiencing apocalyptic visions. He gathered round him followers and adherents, many of whom were extremely young women.

There was great opposition to his teachings and this led to court cases, accusations of immorality and a divided community. It was unknown in the India of the 1930s to allow women to have any say in their own lives, and the teachings are still considered extremely radical in some quarters.

For 14 years the group lived in seclusion, then moved to Mount Abu in Rajasthan where they established their headquarters, and began to disseminate the teachings in other parts of India. In the 1970s they came to the West and the movement grew rapidly. At the time of writing, the University is headed by 96-year old Dadi Janki, one of its very early members. She has dedicated her entire life to the service of God and overseen the establishment of centers and retreats all over the world.

From its shaky beginnings, the University is now highly respected in India, where it has established hospitals, schools and many outreach programmes. Major events for Heads of State and other dignitaries are regularly held at their large Mount Abu complex. The University holds consultative status at the United Nations, and has offices at the UN building in New York.

Sister Jayanti is the European Director, and is a popular, charismatic speaker in demand all over the world.

Although women remain in overall charge, the movement also attracts many men.

To discover more about the fascinating origins of this unique spiritual movement, read Liz Hodgkinson's *Peace and Purity*, published by Rider, and available from BK websites and centers and Amazon.

Select Bibliography of books quoted or cited in the text.

Armstrong, Karen: *The Gospel According to Woman: Christianity's Creation of the Sex War in the West.* Pan, 1986

Bentley Hart, David: *Atheist Delusions: The Christian Revolution and its Fashionable Enemies,* Yale, 2009.

Bohm, David: *Wholeness and the Implicate Order.* Routledge, 1996

Botton, Alain de: Religion for Atheists (ital), Hamish Hamilton, 2012.

D'Aquili, Eugene G: *The Mystical Mind: Probing the Biology of Religious Experience.* Fortress Press, 1999.

Dawkins, Richard: *The Selfish Gene,* Oxford University Press, 1976
The God Delusion, Houghton Mifflin 2006
The Greatest Show on Earth, Transworld, 2009

Eagleton, Terry: *Reason, Faith and Revolution: Reflections on the God Debate,* Yale, 2009.

Friedan, Betty: *The Feminine Mystique,* WW Norton & Co, 1963

Hitchens, Christopher: *God is not Great: Why Religion Poisons Everything.* Atlantic Books, 2007

Hitchens, Christopher: *Hitch-22: A Memoir.* Atlantic Books, 2010

Jayanti, BK: *God's Healing Power.* Michael Joseph, 2002

Meadows, Donella H, Randers, Jorgen and Meadows, Dennis L: *The Limits to Growth*, first published 1972; updated edition, Chelsea Green, 2004.

Mountford, Brian: *Christian Atheist: Belonging without Believing*. O Books, 2011

Parks, Tim: *Medici Money: Banking, Metaphysics and Art in 15th century Florence*. Profile, 2005

Parks, Tim: *Teach Us to Sit Still*. Harvill Secker, 2010

Steinem, Gloria: *Outrageous Acts and Everybody Rebellions*. Flamingo, 1984. Contains the article, 'If Men Could Menstruate'.

Walsch, Neale Donald: *What God Wants*. Atria, 2005

Wollstonecraft, Mary: *A Vindication of the Rights of Woman*. Penguin edition, 2004

Zens, John: *No Will of My Own: How Patriarchy Smothers Female Dignity and Personhood*. Ekklesia Press, 2011

Circle Books

Circle is a symbol of infinity and unity. It's part of a growing list of imprints, including o-books.net and zero-books.net.

Circle Books aims to publish books in Christian spirituality that are fresh, accessible, and stimulating.

Our books are available in all good English language bookstores worldwide. If you can't find the book on the shelves, then ask your bookstore to order it for you, quoting the ISBN and title. Or, you can order online—all major online retail sites carry our titles.

To see our list of titles, please view www.Circle-Books.com, growing by 80 titles per year.

Authors can learn more about our proposal process by going to our website and clicking on Your Company > Submissions.

We define Christian spirituality as the relationship between the self and its sense of the transcendent or sacred, which issues in literary and artistic expression, community, social activism, and practices. A wide range of disciplines within the field of religious studies can be called upon, including history, narrative studies, philosophy, theology, sociology, and psychology. Interfaith in approach, Circle Books fosters creative dialogue with non-Christian traditions.

And tune into MySpiritRadio.com for our book review radio show, hosted by June-Elleni Laine, where you can listen to authors discussing their books.

MySpiritRadio